The Christian Creed

Hans-Werner Schroeder

The Christian Creed

A Meditative Path

Floris Books

Translated by James Hindes

First published in German under the title
Das christliche Bekenntnis. Ein Übungsweg
by Verlag Urachhaus, Stuttgart, 1982.
First published in English in 1985 by Floris Books.

© 1982 Verlag Urachhaus Johannes Mayer
GmbH & Co KG Stuttgart

British Library Cataloguing in Publication Data

Schroeder, Hans-Werner
The Christian creed: a meditative path.
1. Creeds
I. Title   II. Das christliche Bekenntnis. *English*
238   BT990

ISBN 0-86315-032-2

Printed in Great Britain
by Billing & Sons Ltd, Worcester

Contents

1
Understanding
Faith
Confession

1.1 Human existence — Christian existence

As soon as we awaken from the dream of childhood and raise ourselves to a more wakeful consciousness, our life is filled with many questions. Neither science nor tradition can give us satisfactory answers. No source outside of us can. These questions arise within our soul in manifold forms — challenging, pressing, even threatening; but they also awaken longings and a dim awareness that answers must exist somewhere. They drive us to search, to strive and reach beyond our previous experience and knowledge. We often seek to suppress them but then they sink into unconsciousness, only to return later when they weigh even more heavily in our hearts. We can dodge them with a variety of superficial distractions. We can anesthetize ourselves with pleasure, which can go as far as the use of drugs, or we can plunge ourselves into unrelenting activity. Yet we will never succeed in rooting them out of our hearts, for they originate in a place where our innermost being is rooted in the spirit.

Fundamental among these essential questions are the following: What is the meaning of life, of suffering and of death? What assurance do we have that our life and destiny are a part of a larger whole? What is our relationship to God? What is the origin of genuine joy in life? What can we really do with our lives? What is our true relationship to our fellow men and to the various communities of which we are a part? This is only a partial list of the questions that could be mentioned here.

If we were merely creatures of the earth, such questions would not live within us as powerfully as they do. We should be satisfied with the conditions we find on earth. It would never occur to us then that all our experiences might point to a meaning at work in our lives. We should never think that we must ask questions leading beyond the borders of birth and death. These questions live in us because we belong not merely to the earth but also to a higher world from which we originate.

In that world before we were born we beheld our future destiny and the meaning of our lives. We experienced our connection with God and felt a security and a certainty about life which the world of earth can never offer. On earth with our forces we seek anew that which we experienced in the spiritual world as a gift. A certainty given to us without any effort on our part. The unconscious memories of those experiences in preearthly spiritual existence live on in the fundamental questions of our heart. They cause us to inquire and seek beyond the borders of earthly life. The urgency in our heart cannot be silenced until we can at least hope to find and begin to follow the *path* to the answers. The strength of our humanity, our power to realize uniquely *human* goals, is, in large measure, dependent upon the answers. To conclude that these cannot be found would have far-reaching effects upon all my inner striving and for the realization of the truest aims in my life as a *human* being. It would call for a deep resignation. But if, on an inner path, I can hope to find answers filled with vitality, then my life will be permeated with resoluteness and courage. I shall be able to be a better human being on the earth.

The answers stemming from Christianity come from contact with the reality of the spiritual world which we once experienced as our preearthly home. In the Creed these answers have been 'condensed', one could say, into conceptual form, into thoughts, ideas which can lead us not only to being Christian, but also to our true humanity. They can guide us to fulfill the striving we have brought with us from our preearthly existence; we find true meaning given to our earthly existence.

There is yet another place where the answers to the questions our heart asks can be found: in ritual, in the sacraments. Here the reality of the spirit is not merely grasped and expressed in thoughts as it is in the Creed but rather the reality of the spirit itself, *as it works in the world*, comes close to us. In sacramental actions the world from which we originate lives in a real and effective way. We encounter the forces which created us, the divine ground of our inception. By uniting our earthly being and struggles with the spiritual reality which comes to meet us in the sacraments we form within us a power which enables us not only to know, but actually to experience the answers to our life questions.

Therefore we find in Christianity two sources for these, the Creed and ritual.

Spirit reality as revealed to understanding is made available to us by the power at work in the Creed and can then lead us from understanding to living faith and to a confession of our faith. In ritual the nearness of the spirit works directly upon us. Its power gives our own efforts and understanding the necessary complement of empirical, living experience. Through its working it urgently asks to be grasped with understanding. The two

11

sources complete one another. Therefore, it is proper for
the Creed to be spoken within Christian religious
services, where it serves as a summary of all that which
can be experienced in a living way in the ritual.

We do not need to give up hope for answers to the
deep questions of our human existence. To be sure, they
do not come in an intellectual way. The very depth of
the questions demands deep experience of the world and
if he can open his heart to it, this is close to man in
ritual itself. We gradually come closer to realizing the
ideal of true humanity is rapidly declining in our time.
In times past it was given to many people in a natural
way. Through their actions these people showed they
instinctively knew how to be *human* beings. But that
talent is dying out. As with many other things today,
this ability must be acquired anew, usually with great
effort, by each individual.

A Christianity which is not based on empty or not-
understood dogmas but is able to lead man to a living
experience of spiritual reality will also be in a position
to open paths leading to that reality. In the Creed shine
the starry heavens of those truths, which may become
for us living pictures leading to true humanity on earth.

1.2　The Creed and the reality of the spirit

The sentences which we find in the Creed, Christianity's statement of faith, are a precipitate of the experiences which mankind had in earlier encounters with the spiritual reality of the world. An ancient wisdom shines in these sentences which was revealed through insights into the spiritual reality. During the development of Christianity the formulations of the Creed underwent a gradual evolution as those experiences were stated in an often controversial step-by-step process. Still, it was not merely theological-philosophical considerations which were involved; at the decisive moments of the Church councils, in the thinking of the early Church fathers, the wisdom which still often originated in the background of the mysteries was summed up in fixed concepts.

Therefore when we turn to the sentences of the Creed we can feel we are walking on solid spiritual ground. Certainly the old forms of the Creed, the Apostles' or the Nicene Creed, from the first Christian centuries, do present us with certain difficulties today. These formulations arose at a time when mankind was much closer to the spirit than it is today, when the truth of the Creed was easier to verify in the first place. In prayer, in reflecting on the Gospels, and above all in ritual it was much easier then for the human soul to be enlightened by those experiences which enabled his heart to say, 'I believe in God', or which made it possible to sense and feel redemption and grace through Jesus Christ.

Today we are not given this experience. The Creed has taken on a new form, which includes all the truths already witnessed in the old creeds; but the formulation of these truths is new and appropriate for our present and future possibilities of experience. There lives in this new form the original spirit, the original depth of spiritual experience. Hence, we can count on a solid foundation in the renewed Creed also. At the same time we can expect to find depths of wisdom which would not be revealed to superficial understanding.

1.3 Can I understand the statements of Christianity?

Does our assertion that the sentences of the Creed have profound depths imply, as traditional Christianity maintains, that Christian truths are only to be believed and not understood? Must we sacrifice our own thinking in order to achieve faith as if the 'statements of faith' stood in crass contradiction to the statements of reason?

These questions must be answered with a clear 'No'. In this little book I have not set myself the task of making the Creed accessible to modern understanding and consciousness. Such an undertaking would be more in the province of theology and philosophy. Much has been done to this end; the results can be found in the literature of The Christian Community, for example in the works of Emil Bock.

If our view of the world expands to include the earthly and the spiritual in equal measure, then it is possible to find reasonable, enlightening insights into such difficult subjects as: creation, the Trinity, Resurrection, and life after death. This is possible today through the science of the spirit developed by Rudolf Steiner, which provides secure foundations for a Christian conception of the world. From an understanding of the world which encompasses both heaven and earth, it is possible to grasp the truths of Christianity anew.

At the same time, understanding leads to an

experience of the truth; it opens the heart. That this can be so is not obvious, for all merely intellectual understanding runs the risk of paralyzing man's ability to experience deeply. If I 'understand' that man and nature are only explainable as an accidental collection of atoms and molecules, then my view and experience of *all* of reality begins to darken. Such an understanding excludes the spiritual reality which lives in both man and nature. On the other hand there is another 'understanding' which is able to think of man and nature as permeated, ever created, by spirit and which is just as clear, precise and logical as the other means of knowing. It can even include atoms and molecules as parts of the full reality.

We are speaking of just such a spiritual understanding and knowing when we point to the possibility of not merely *believing* in the Creed, accepting the sentences as dogmas. That kind of believing was both necessary and possible in past ages of Christianity when thinking was not yet predominant in our experience of the world. Today, however, it is possible to penetrate the Creed with understanding. Here new paths can be followed which lead into a deep comprehension of spiritual reality.

This little book is addressed to readers who, following such paths, have begun once again to feel they can trust the truths of Christianity. With this as starting point we should like to point to the steps which lead beyond understanding to confessing in daily life. In doing so (*because* we have involved our thinking) we touch on a realm which in religious life has always been called faith.

1.4 *If I understand, do I then have to believe?*

The word faith is usually taken to mean an uncertain accepting as true something which cannot be known exactly; for example, 'I believe tomorrow will be a beautiful day.'

But something else entirely is meant when we say 'I believe in this person!' Then belief designates an inner activity, not arrived at unthinkingly but spoken concerning an individual at a decisive moment in his life. Then the word points to two things: First, that I have *perceived* the essential character traits of the other person so that I can believe in him; a deeper relationship comes into play, not based on mere external facts but grounded in an inner, intuitive grasp of the other person. Secondly, the word 'belief' means a personal confession of faith in the other, a personal stance taken with respect to him. This commitment goes beyond mere perception and understanding.

If in looking at a child, a teacher says 'I believe in him,' far more is expressed than if he had merely said: 'I know him, I understand him.' Here knowing (for example, knowing certain aspects of a pupil's character) and understanding are included. But above and beyond mere knowing there lives in the words 'I believe in him' an active trust that the pupil is capable of a positive development of his capacities.

This double nuance — a deeper perception and a

personal acknowledgment, a personal stance taken toward the perceived — leads to the only meaning which can be intended in the religious sense with this word. In genuine faith there lives an intuition of certainty concerning connections which cannot be grasped in any external sense. For this reason Emil Bock, a founder and one of the leading personalities in The Christian Community, occasionally translated the word 'faith' with the expression 'the power of the heart to see'; there is a power at work in faith which can intuitively grasp deeper connections and essences. One *can* see with the heart. Above and beyond this, however, faith is not only perception, it also changes things: it leads to an inner, personal union with that in which one believes. If someone really 'believes' in God, then it will become visible how he trusts his destiny, even in his daily actions; otherwise the powers which live within faith have not yet unfolded.

We could also call this power which lives in faith a mutual binding. This mutual binding is already indicated in the words, 'I believe in this pupil'; the teacher places himself, so to speak, on the side of the pupil. The bond is even stronger when we say, 'I believe in God'. If words are to be true, then they must have consequences for the other parts of my life. They contain more than if I just say, 'I understand that God must exist'; or, 'I know that God exists'. If 'I believe *in* God', I step on to the side of him in whom faith is expressed. I unite myself inwardly with him. I step over to him, so to speak, with my inner existence.

This side of faith begins to work when I find myself in inner crises or outer dangers. It can then be seen whether or not I have reached a state of faith which really unites me with the divine and gives me strength to carry through; this kind of strength always dwells within faith when it is deep enough. This little book is written to awaken and develop this 'strength to carry through.' So the question, 'How can I understand?' will only be touched on here inasmuch as context requires. Our concern is: 'If that which is expressed in the Creed is true, then what does it signify for my life?' We are moving from the question of knowing to that of life itself, of human existence; in other words from knowledge to acknowledgment, to a confession of faith with its inner sense of a self-imposed obligation.

Thus it becomes clear what adding faith to knowledge means. Although I may slowly learn to know that God exists, still it could take a long time before I believe in him. Michael Bauer, an esoteric pupil of Rudolf Steiner once said, 'The devil also knows that god exists but he doesn't believe in him.' Let us consider again our example from everyday life. A teacher can know and understand his pupils — but to believe in them requires a deeper engagement. In the realm of religion, this bond *must* join up with mere knowledge about spiritual things — only then can that which we think we know about God, Christ, redemption, and so on, become active and fruitful for our life. And even our knowing acquires an authentic relationship to life when the heart is also engaged.

We live in a time when it is again possible to know much concerning the spiritual world and the beings within it. But the danger exists that we allow this new knowledge to lack the necessary involvement. We may know but we do not believe what we know; and in the end the knowledge itself will lose its power. We are attempting here to indicate several paths by which this

19

danger can be overcome with respect to the fundamental truths of Christianity.

On the other hand, it should be borne clearly in mind: Without a genuine knowledge of the spiritual world today, even the power of faith would be lost; a 'mere' and 'blind' faith *cannot* be sufficient for today. Without the support of a genuine knowledge concerning the spiritual world, the active power of faith which lives in every human being will inevitably degenerate into superstition or, as is so often in evidence today, something worse.

Authentic knowledge of the spirit opens the heart for the power of faith; it gives faith certainty, it gives the light necessary for the 'power of the heart to see'. It makes faith, the involvement of the deepest, innermost part of the human being, possible again.

1.5 Faith: the effects of confession in life

Up to this point we have used the terms 'faith' and 'confession' or 'confession of faith' without explicitly distinguishing between them; they are indeed closely related. A more precise distinction can, however, now lead us a bit further.

In the earliest centuries of Christianity confessing to the Christian faith was often mortally dangerous. Innumerable people were killed because of their faith. They often could have avoided death simply by acknowledging the state religion. Although some followed that path, most died for their confession of faith, thereby 'sealing' their faith.

Would we have the strength to do something like that today? Perhaps the question lacks relevance in view of the safe, 'guaranteed' conditions in which we think we live today. But just a glance at the conditions in the Communist-bloc countries and other parts of the earth can bring this question to life for us. How strong is our profession of faith in Christ? Has it become so mature, so inwardly certain, that it could hold up under any test of destiny?

Perhaps what is intended with this question is now clear: Faith, as we have already seen, has by its very nature an inner sense of connectedness, a feeling of 'belonging together' which might even be experienced as a sense of self-imposed feeling of obligation. This aspect

21

of faith speaks of a strength in the will which leads by its inner nature to an act of avowing, declaring, professing or confessing a faith. Of course, it is also noticeable that this strength of the will at work in faith can be stronger or weaker; strong enough or not strong enough to hold us upright in a moment of mortal danger.

In our relationship to religious truth we can distinguish three steps, which are simultaneously three regions of our soul:

Understanding the truths of Christianity	– Thinking
Uniting with them — Faith	– Heart
Confessing to them	– Will.

Confession begins where faith takes hold of the will and awakens in it the power to act to shape our life according to our faith.

First of all, two things must be stressed here: by 'confession in life' we do not mean any kind of 'oral confession', as if one had to give expression to his faith with words as often as possible; of course, occasionally this can be just what is needed. However, our stance in life works much more powerfully, often without many words, particularly in little things. Secondly, this sequence 'understanding, faith, confession' is in no way intended as the actual inner steps of the soul. Often it happens that our heart is touched by a truth and the power of faith is thereby awakened; then comes the additional step of striving to understand what one feels in order to achieve certainty from the understanding and, out of that, to unfold the courage to avow or confess one's faith.

The elemental will within man to confess to the Good and the True, sometimes provides the first step and pulls the other steps along after it. What we here distinguish in three steps of soul life, in actual life weaves together with each part influencing the other two.

We began above with the — admittedly extreme — situation of a death threat in order to make the power of a confession of faith as clear as possible. Now we can return to day-to-day life since the Christian mood of soul must meet not only in extreme situations but also entirely mundane daily affairs. In certain respects it is much more difficult to maintain a confessing faith in God on a day-to-day basis than, perhaps, in an extreme situation of destiny, in which we must call up all our strength. For then we usually also have special help from the spiritual world. Confession of faith in our life means: in every situation, in the moods of everyday life, on the job, in the family, in the little wars with our fellow human beings — that we stand as a Christian in all these situations. It is hard. We see right away that it is impossible. We can't do it. But we can practice, striving toward actual accomplishment. The Creed itself can become a path to develop the power of our faith.

1.6   The Creed as a path

It is hard to maintain the basic Christian attitudes towards others and life in day-to-day life. On the other hand, it is precisely this which is intended if we seriously want to travel down the road which leads to becoming a Christian, to *being* a Christian. This requires the little steps which are taken day by day.

A child that is to grow up under our care requires regular, loving attention. Our existence as Christians, the life of the Christian spirit within us, is still as weak and undeveloped as a small child; likewise it requires daily cultivation and faithful efforts for us to mature and become stronger: prayer, reading the Bible and the ritual of religious services are the most important religious means for this purpose. The study of the Creed is a further item on this list.

A new form of the Creed is read in the central sacrament of The Christian Community, the Act of Consecration of Man. It is given a person for regular use when he or she becomes a member. It is not thereby intended that anyone who actively takes the Creed into his spiritual life should already 'believe' all of the truths therein contained; but daily reflection on these truths will enable them to serve as guiding principles in life. The daily occupation with the Creed can bring about a constantly renewed dedication to the divine aims of mankind. In the twelve sentences of the Creed we find something like a spiritual sky filled with stars with which we can orientate our lives.

Here we would like to point out an essential difference between the traditional forms of the Creed and the Creed of The Christian Community. All older forms of the Creed begin with the phrase 'I believe', or 'we believe'. These words actually gave the Creed its original name, for the Latin *credo* means 'I believe.' Other words in English used to designate the summary of fundamental Christian truths are 'confession' and 'confession of faith.' In the renewed form of the Creed, as it is used in The Christian Community, the phrase 'I believe' is absent. Instead of 'I believe in . . .' there is a clear statement in all sentences, for instance, 'An almighty divine being *is* . . .' 'Then he overcame . . .'

Here the Creed does not start from the standpoint of faith; rather, statements about fact, truths are placed before us. We can look up to these truths and then, with time, through use of our freedom and understanding, we can find our own relationship to them. Through understanding, the path opens to believing and then to confessing the Creed. This relationship can also be deepened daily. Through daily use of the Creed we gradually attain to a deeper understanding; sentences formerly not understood or understood only vaguely, become deep and clear; others, to which we had access from the beginning, acquire new, altered or additional meanings.

But that is not all; for, above all, we can ask ourselves every day anew: *What does this word, this sentence mean for my life?* If God is: then how must my life be shaped: If Christ overcame death: what relationship can I have to death? If we pose questions in this way, the

25

Creed becomes a daily exercise; it becomes a very real *path*.

On the path we gradually achieve the maturity for our existence as Christians and a guiding strength for our lives. For, as we have seen, these twelve sentences are not an accidental collection of arbitrary truths. They arise (already in the old form of the Apostolic Creed) from a genuine knowledge concerning the spiritual depths of Christianity and its relationship to man.

It is, of course, clear that the deeper truths of the world cannot be discussed with superficial words. Hence, the sentences of the Creed do not reveal their deeper meaning with the first superficial hearing. Every word in these sentences has its own weight and far-reaching meaning. And yet the sentences are clearly formed, surveyable, and accessible to understanding.

The fundamental truths of human existence are summarized in an extremely succinct fashion. They can accompany us through our entire lives and lead us in an ongoing deepening of experience.

What do the fundamental truths of Christianity mean for my life? The larger part of this book will concern itself with this question. All twelve sentences will be examined from this point of view. The concluding chapter will present suggestions for daily work with the Creed.

2
The significance of the basic truths of Christianity

The Creed of The Christian Community

An almighty divine being, spiritual-physical, is the ground of existence of the heavens and of the earth who goes before his creatures like a Father.

Christ, through whom men attain the re-enlivening of the dying earth-existence, is to this divine being as the Son born in eternity.

In Jesus the Christ entered as man into the earthly world.

The birth of Jesus upon earth is a working of the Holy Spirit who, to heal spiritually the sickness of sin of the bodily nature of mankind, prepared the son of Mary to be the vehicle of the Christ.

The Christ Jesus suffered under Pontius Pilate the death on the cross and was lowered into the grave of the earth.

In death he became the helper of the souls of the dead who had lost their divine nature.

Then he overcame death after three days.

Since that time he is the Lord of the heavenly forces upon earth and lives as the fulfiller of the fatherly deeds of the ground of the world.

He will in time unite for the advancement of the world with those whom, through their bearing, he can wrest from the death of matter.

Through him can the healing Spirit work.

Communities whose members feel the Christ within themselves may feel united in a Church to which all belong who are aware of the health-bringing power of the Christ.

They may hope for the overcoming of the sickness of sin; for the continuance of man's being; and for the preservation of their life destined for eternity.

We now turn to an individual discussion of each of the twelve sentences. Each chapter will examine first what a particular sentence of the Creed is saying, and then the question of its significance for our lives.

2.1 Sheltered in the Father

The first sentence reads: *An almighty divine being, spiritual-physical is the ground of existence of the heavens and of the earth who goes before his creatures like a Father.* God is here referred to as the ground of all existence; the ground of existence of *all* beings, of *all* worlds. Yet he is also the ground of my individual life and being, a foundation upon which I can stand. Just as the firm ground of the earth underneath my feet lends my bodily existence a firm certainty, so too is the ground of my entire being in God. I feel a firm security a 'being grounded' in the final unshakable ground of the world. Thus, no matter what may happen, my being *in its fundamental ground* cannot be shaken.

Furthermore this ultimate ground of my existence of my being, is 'spiritual-physical'. One can easily be offended if this formulation is taken so that the word physical is equated with the word material. What is intended with the juxtaposition of the two concepts, spiritual and physical, becomes clear when we consider that the divine must be thought of as carrying and working in all areas of the world. Ultimately, all realms of existence are permeated by him, heavenly and earthly, spiritual and physical: he does not have only spiritual existence but works also within the earthly, maintaining and shaping. So I can awaken within myself the feeling that my entire being, not only soul and spirit, but also my body, has its ground in God. As a *full* human being

I am included in the being of the divine, even in the depths of my bodily existence. Not that any kind of divinity should be attributed to matter itself, but the forces which organize, shape and maintain everything material as having their final ground in the existence of God, not in anonymous laws.

From the words 'ground of existence' there can arise a profoundly deep trust that the divine in the world holds sway in my own being, even in my bodily existence. Something of this archetypal feeling, a feeling that rises up from the deepest intuitions we have concerning life, something of this archetypal trust in the divine, lives in the song which Martin Luther wrote: The words 'A solid fortress is our God' have given the hearts of Christians courage and confidence for centuries. The word 'ground' contains a second meaning. It means not only 'foundation', but also 'cause' or 'reason'. For example, 'grounds for some action'. This meaning does not answer the question of the final ground of our *spatial* existence, the final *thing* upon which everything is based, but rather it answers the 'why' of our existence.

Why am I anyway? And why is the world? And why is anything anyway? The 'grounds for', or the reason for the being of the world and for my own existence lies in God. Not in any accident. Not in an accidental conglomeration of atoms and molecules. Not merely in a series of ancestors leading up to me. Not in a sequence of events which may have come together accidentally and are beyond my ability to understand. Not in impenetrable blows of destiny. My ground is in God. He is the cause of my life and my 'I', but also the cause of the world.

The first meaning of the word ground leads to a feeling of existential certainty and to trust, faith. The second meaning leads to the beginning of an awareness that all life must be created and formed, caused by a divine meaning, that all life is filled with sense which comes from God, and that this divine meaning gives shape and significance to my own personal existence.

Yet there is another, a third, meaning contained in the first sentence of the Creed which we would like to discuss, 'who goes before his creatures like a Father.' With the word 'Father' is indicated that, in this ground of being, I do not have an impersonal something before me to which no direct relationship is possible, but rather I have a being who presents himself in a personal way, who, in the highest sense of the word, can be experienced as a 'father', who goes before. This means not only that I can turn to the Godhead in a personal way but also that the Godhead can turn to me and feel with me, care for me with love. The word fatherly describes his behavior.

So we can hear the words of Christ, 'your heavenly father knows that you need . . . all [these things]' (Matt. 6:32). Here he means all the things that cause us cares and worries. In the Book of Revelation we find the words, God 'will wipe away every tear from their eyes' (21:4). This is indeed a very sublime picture for the fatherliness of God.

In the words 'going before' we have again a double meaning. First of all, they mean walking ahead. But there is also the sense of being 'ahead of', or preceding in time. With respect to time, the father moves ahead of the son. So, the divine goes ahead of all beings as their creator. It is 'earlier' in its 'Being' than that which then, as creature, goes forth from it. The direction in which all creation is headed is the direction in which God is to be found. He got there 'first' so to speak.

If that is so, what does it mean for our lives? If it is true that in God all being and existence has its ground, if God bears and penetrates everything, then is my being and everything which I experience also grounded and borne within him. Then it is also true that I can never in any way 'fall out' of this divine being. No matter what happens to me, wherever I may go, no matter how I may lose myself, for all joys and all pain, there is a deep ground, a ground of existence. He himself provides the very foundation for the existence of any abyss, for the divine would not be the ground of all being if there were *anything* which was not grounded in it.

And this applies above all to the particular destiny which I must carry. Nothing can happen that could possibly have the power to tear me away from the might of God, no matter where I might fall. If I only look deeply enough I will again find God in the depths, in the deepest foundations of my situation. Even the most painful suffering, if I properly grasp it, cannot distance me from God. Perhaps this is something my consciousness may refuse to acknowledge or not be able to understand. However, in the deepest grounds of my existence this truth can be experienced within the heart.

Even evil must then serve the good. It takes a stand against the working of the divine and yet it cannot do otherwise than intensify, through resistance, the effectiveness of the good. Paul touches on this secret in his Letter to the Romans (8:38f) when he says 'For I am sure that neither death, nor life, nor angels, nor principalities, nor things present, nor things to come, nor powers, nor height, nor depth, nor anything else in all creation, will be able to separate us from the love of God in Christ Jesus our Lord.' Paul's own experience of the fatherly ground of the world resonates in a wonderful way in these words. And Paul in his dramatic and often incredibly difficult destiny can say in his Letter to the Romans, 'For I am *sure*'. Here the Greek word for 'sure' is *pépeismai*, which means persuaded or having been persuaded *through experience*. These words which can be found in the Letter to the Romans do not arise from an idealistic conception of the divine. They are the result of Paul's painful life experience.

If this word concerning the ground of existence of the heavens and of the earth and his fatherliness is true, then I can feel myself completely borne up and protected within this ground. Then I do not need ever or anywhere to despair in the cares of life. Then I do not need in the end, to have any more fear of anything. For then I will be able to say to myself *wherever I may go*, the Godhead, that is to say, the divine, has been there before me, caring like a Father. And even when I am forced to suffer, perhaps I will be able to accept it as something from God and to experience it as something from his hand with a special meaning intended for me.

Here our work with the Creed leads us to one of the most significant feelings which a Christian can have. The feeling of being borne up, carried within the final being of the Divine. Every fear loses its meaning when placed next to this deep feeling. Every fear is gradually dissolved by this faith which has been grounded in the Divine that carries all existence.

Nietzsche once said that he could not believe Christianity because 'Christians would have to appear to me more redeemed'. In the same sense we must say, 'Christians should have fewer fears'. This is where faith in God must prove itself.

Of course, such certainty of faith is not created itself from one day to the next. It can only be the slowly ripening fruit of a deepening of the religious spirit over a long period of time. But perhaps just here we find that the Creed can serve us. Perhaps in the Creed lies the power to awaken and bring forth the forces in us which we need in order to become Christians.

We can direct our attention to the first sentence of the Creed, perhaps in the morning for a period, or for a week, or through an entire month. We need for this only a few moments. We take these words into ourselves and permeate ourselves with the feeling of the Godhead who works in a fatherly way. We can undertake to return to this feeling again and again through the day and in those decisive moments which otherwise would release discord and fear we attempt to immerse ourselves entirely in it.

In the evening we can look back over the day and ask how much of that which we took upon ourselves in the morning have we actually been able to realize. It will perhaps be very little. But we should not expect at the beginning to achieve everything which can really only be acquired after long practice. Otherwise, we wouldn't need such exercises. What is of importance is rather a faithful daily struggle for the spiritual goals which want to work into our lives and transform them. Then gradually it will become noticeable how our practice finds its way into everyday experiences and feelings.

The first basic Christian feeling is: Trust in the Father God — he is the ground of all existence, also of my life and my destiny. He works like a father, going ahead. I am protected in the divine.

2.2 Christ — our life and the life of the world

The second sentence reads: *Christ, through whom men attain the re-enlivening of the dying earth-existence, is to this divine being as the Son born in eternity.*

With a mighty stride the Creed leads from the experience of the Father to the experience of Christ, of the Son. Only one sentence, though, as we have seen, one filled with a powerful content, is dedicated to the Father God. (In the eighth sentence the Father motif appears again, but then related to Christ, who is spoken of as 'the fulfiller of the fatherly deeds of the ground of the world'.) In comparison, the working of the Son is allocated eight sentences. Now we are no longer dealing with the ground and the foundation of the world but with the creative deeds 'born' out of the ground of existence, which carry over into life and destiny. This is the sphere of the Son.

That God has a son, is the mark of distinction between Christianity and Islam.* It is experienced as a blasphemy in Islam to attribute a son to God, indeed to think of him entangled in any kind of 'family relationship'. What can it then mean if, in Christianity, the existence of God's son is spoken of with equal emphasis? Of course, we should not forget that our earthly consciousness can only employ earthly pictures

* See *Christianity and Islam* by Rudolf Frieling.

to represent spiritual conditions and relationships extending far beyond our everyday consciousness. These pictures can never perfectly correspond to reality. They are only able to *point* to the spiritual reality. This fact appears in the little word 'as', in the phrase 'as the Son born in eternity.' What is expressed in these words enables us to see the creative rejuvenating power which goes forth from the Godhead. Within our experience of God we can find not only eternal peace, the ground which carries us, that is, the experience of the Father; but also from this eternally peaceful ground, out of the fullness of his being, there goes forth something like a powerful spring of creative life. This is the world of the Son. Resting in the peace of the eternal ground, the Father creates through the Son the fullness of life and all creatures. Through the Son he gives existence and development to other beings. He sets in motion a world of unfolding development.

This difference between the Father God and the Son God comes to expression in a monumental way in the words: 'The Father God be in us, the Son God create in us'. The world would be forced to endure in a frozen state of eternal rigidity, as we see for example in the majesty of high mountains made of granite, which serve us as a picture for the tranquillity and eternal power of the Father ground, if it were not for the power of the Son that is born from the Father. It is the becoming, the blossoming of the world that arises through this birth. In the experience of springtime we can sense and feel the forces of eternal becoming and blossoming which, in addition to the powers of peaceful eternal being are also present in the world. In springtime beautiful and life-filled images for the kingdom and the working of the Son God come to meet us. And still they are only weak transitory pictures for the eternally new, creative powers of Christ.

With the Son God the Father 'extends beyond himself.' The Son makes it possible for the world to go further so that 'the same' and 'the one' are not eternally all there is in existence, so that development and unfolding are possible and so that at the end of time, there can be more and other kinds of being than in the beginning.

In the prologue of John's Gospel, the creative power of the Son is called the Logos, the Word. It is said there, 'all things were made through him, and without him was not anything made that was made.' And Paul points to the same mystery when he writes: 'for in him all things were created, in heaven and on earth, visible and invisible, whether thrones or dominions or principalities or authorities — all things were created through him and for him.' (Col.1:16).

Now, however, in the second sentence of the Creed there is a clause added which includes in a surprising way the opposite of life: a reference to the dying earth existence, 'Christ through whom men attain the re-enlivening of the dying earth existence.' It is interesting that this reference is altogether missing in the old forms of the Creed. Until recently it was not possible for mankind to stand face to face in such an elementary way as often happens today with the earthly forces of death.

This is not the place to discuss the entry of the forces of death into world history and the history of mankind. They are there and they are at work. Everywhere we experience them today: in the earth, in our fellow human beings, in ourselves. They have been at work since the time when the paradisical condition of the world ended through the fall into sin. Since then, the earth has been getting old. The forces of death

39

overshadow the sunlike paradisical forces of life which came from the beginning.

Novalis in his *Hymns to The Night* (V) has described this transition as follows:

> To its end inclined
> The Ancient World.
> The happy garden
> Of the youthful race
> Withered away;
> Out into freer spaces
> Strove the full grown
> Unchildlike mankind.
> Vanished were the Gods;
> Lonely and lifeless
> Stood nature,
> Robbed of her soul
> By strict number
> And iron chains.
> Laws arose,
> And in ideas
> As in dust and air
> Fell to pieces
> The measureless prime
> Of the thousand-fold life.
> Fled away
> Was all-powerful Faith
> And Fantasy,
> All transforming,
> All uniting,
> Heavenly comrade.
> Unfriendly blew
> A cold North wind
> Over the frozen plains,

And the wonderland home
Passed away in the Ether.
. . .
No longer was Light,
the abode of the Gods,
and a heavenly token —
Around them they drew
The curtain of Night.

In a wonderful way these words characterize the forces of death taking hold of all of existence. In the Old Testament the expulsion from paradise through the working of the serpent is described in a similar way. Man is made subject to death and the fields of earth are cursed.

By considering the process of aging in man we can grasp this development of death in its tragedy and, at the same time, in its significance for the world. For the intervention of the forces of death also has meaning. A young child still lives in a very natural way within the paradisical forces of existence. It is, however, still without any development of personality, any unfolding of the self. If consciousness and awareness of self are to become effective in the life of the individual, then he must grow old and in so doing, lose the forces of childhood. He must take upon himself death and the possibility of sickness and weakness. But just through this experience the human being acquires the ability to find himself again in a higher way and with it comes also the possibility of giving himself consciously to the world. Loss becomes gain.

We can regard in the same way the aging and dying of the earth existence, in which mankind participates. It has a deep significance for the maturation of humanity and at the same time there lies a great tragedy and danger in it. Novalis said this with these accurate words: 'Out into freer spaces/Strove the full grown/Unchildlike mankind.' Space has become free but desolate; human beings have become unchildlike. But they have also grown up to their higher destination and an inner freedom which could not be given them in the condition of childhood. So we regard the consequences of the fall into sin as a process of aging and a possibility for development.

The Creed speaks in the second sentence not only about the dying earth existence but also about the re-enlivening through Christ and his powers of creation: 'Christ, through whom men attain the re-enlivening of the dying earth-existence'. How does Christ work into the powers of death in earth existence? How does he work against those powers?

This question leads us to the significance which the events of Christianity hold for the whole world. Again, we can achieve a better understanding by observing the aging of human beings; for the destiny of man is not threatened by death for the first time in old age. At an earlier age, sickness can intervene, or an accident can happen which leads to death.

There is a point on the path of mankind's development concerning which modern science of the spirit must say: Actually, human life on earth should have come to an end at that time since the natural forces of life on earth and of human bodies were exhausted. The effects of the forces of death since the Fall from paradise had already then reached a first high point and if nothing else had occurred, would have led mankind through a deep penetrating decadence, a radical atrophy of its existence on earth. There would, indeed, still have been human bodies on earth, however, they would no longer have been able to serve as a dwelling place for the human ego.

Rudolf Steiner describes* how humanity was threatened with extinction through the decay of the body.

> ... at about the time of the Mystery of Golgotha the human physical body had reached a degree of decline where ... [human beings] were faced with the danger of leaving an earth that was growing more and more desolate and barren, and of finding no possibility in the future of descending from the world of spirit-and-soul.
>
> ... Mankind was rescued from this fate through that which was achieved by the Mystery of Golgotha whereby the human physical body itself was imbued again with the necessary forces of life and freshness. Men were thereby enabled to continue their further evolution on earth, inasmuch as they could now come down from the worlds of spirit-and-soul and find it possible to live in physical bodies. Such was the actual effect of the Mystery of Golgotha.

This stage of development arrived around the time of Christ. Why was it necessary for Christ to appear at this point in time? One possible answer to this question is: The effects of the adversary powers' forces of death threatened to get the upper hand.

The decadence which was spreading rapidly, even into the bodily nature of mankind, became visible in the decay of forces in the Roman culture. In the personalities of the Caesars it was quite palpable, for example, in Tiberius or Nero. Also figures such as Cleopatra or

---

* Lecture of May 7, 1923 in *Ascension and Pentecost*.

Herod shared all the signs of decadence. The mysteries of antiquity lost their strength. The old rituals had become ineffective and some had even decayed to the point where they had become instruments for demonic forces, as in the fertility cults of the Near East. Also other rituals, originally cults of healing, had fallen into decay. The widespread appearance of leprosy in Asia-Minor was also a symptom of the decay of physical bodies.

Educated people of that time spoke with a consciousness of the descent of mankind from a golden age down to a silver age and then into an iron age. The time of a distance from the spirit and the threat of death had come. A widespread expectation of a redeemer who would reverse this descent of mankind was to be found everywhere.

All of this lives in a particularly impressive way in a folk which, externally at least, was perhaps the least touched by decay: in the Germanic tribes and their mythology. Here the consciousness of the dying of the old forces of mankind, the consciousness of the descent of the world and its gods, is portrayed in the twilight of the gods. The Germanic gods suffered defeat in battle with the powers of the adversary — the wolf, the snake. And with that, the world as it existed until then, went under. With a tremendous realism this mood of world downfall lived in the Germanic peoples. They did not look merely upon external events with these pictures. Above all inner processes were seen in which the all-encompassing crisis in man's forces of life were experienced.

To meet this, there came through Christ a powerful stream of life-forces, of renewing, enlivening, rejuvenating forces into the world of earth and humanity. By taking death upon himself, entering into death, he was able to illuminate it from within and open a new spring of life for humanity.

Through this, as a first result, life for all of mankind on earth was saved. As every human being is subject to death, every human being benefits from the re-enlivening deed of Christ. Christ died for all humanity, even if not a single individual knows about it.

Because of this Novalis in his *Hymns to The Night* (V) was able to continue, after the description of the entry of the forces of death, with these words concerning the Christ event.

> Thou art that youthful form our tombs display
> Standing above them, deep in contemplation,
> Consoling emblem in our darkest day
> Of higher manhood's joyful new foundation.

Christ appears to Novalis in the picture of a youth. In the first Christian centuries he was portrayed again and again this way.

Of course that did not mean that the end of the drama of life and death had been reached. Through the Christ event a re-enlivening on earth had occurred at that time so that life on earth could continue. This was achieved in principle. We thank the deed of Christ for the fact that we can live and exist as spiritual beings on the earth. We live through his life.

Just as someone who is critically ill can sometimes be saved through a blood transfusion and be equipped with fresh life-forces, so has humanity and the earth, in the highest sense possible, received through the life blood of the Son God a transfusion of divine life-forces which have been introduced into the earth. Mankind can be thankful for this life-saving deed.

However, humanity cannot in the long run be given these life forces as a continual gift. Man's own actions must and should come to meet the deed of God, otherwise man would remain only a receiver and would not be able to contribute anything himself. If that were to happen, then the meaning of humanity's development would be lost. What could fundamentally happen only through the mystery of Golgotha, would have to bring man into a one-sided dependency if he himself were not able to employ these given forces to work together with God at overcoming the forces of death. This lies in the phrase, 'men attain the re-enlivening.'

'Men' is the subject of the sentence; that is, they also must become active. Their active doing is implicit. It is not only that something is being offered as gift. This bestowal by Christ resonates in a wonderful way in the word 'attain.'

The incredible intensification of the forces of death in our time is a challenge to humanity to become aware of the power of Christ that lies within and to take hold of it. That is why Christianity exists on the earth. Everything which happens in a Christian way, allows some of the life forces of Christ to ray forth into the earth and humanity. The sacraments themselves are especially powerful concentrations of these life forces from which new, higher, life constantly flows into the earth and mankind. The more consciously human beings participate in these forces, the more powerfully effective they become. The secret of this higher life in the sacrament is spoken by Christ himself in the institutions of the Lord's Supper on Maundy Thursday, in the words with which he gives his body and his blood, that is, *his life* which he pours into earthly forms. Adding to these words he calls upon his disciples to cultivate his deed further.

Today The Christian Community has been in existence long enough to be able to speak out of experience concerning the effectiveness of the sacramental life. In ritual the enlivening and healing power of Christ comes into direct proximity with the human being. Not only with the human being but also the earth itself receives life forces through the cultivation of ritual. For it is Christ who would lead the life of the entire world into a higher order, but only with the active co-working of human beings.

It was necessary to expand the idea of the re-enlivening of the dying earth existence when speaking of the second sentence of the Creed. It will be necessary to take up this idea again and develop it further in connection with other sentences of the Creed.

We must still say something about the inner connection between the main body of the sentence and the inserted clause: 'Christ, *through whom men attain the re-enlivening of the dying earth-existence*, is to this divine being as the Son born in eternity.' We have spoken about the source of the creative power which comes forth from the Godhead in eternity and is shaped by the Son. It is these creative powers of the Son which then set this power of re-enlivening against the dying of earth existence.

Again we ask: If this is all true, what does it mean for my life, for my consciousness as a Christian?

Two things can occur to us. First of all, the awareness that our lives as human beings on earth are owed to Christ will gradually be transformed into a feeling of a basic unity with Christ: into the feeling 'I could not exist as a human being on the earth, I could not live and strive with my human abilities, if Christ had not,

47

through his deed, created a stream of life that flowed and is still flowing today into the earth. For my personal life and existence is due to Christ's deed, even when I am not aware of it. His sacrifice is my life, even if I do not or cannot live accordingly.' This is expressed in the service, that our life arises out of his creating life, indeed, *is* his life.

The fundamental Christian feeling which can arise in us through the second sentence of the Creed is this: 'We can feel ourselves in our entire human existence in every moment united with Christ, just as the life of a plant is united with the cosmos through the light of the sun and thereby constantly wrested free from the dead realm of minerals.'

But there is a second thing. Through Christ in me I can contribute to the battle for the earth so that the excess of death forces is opposed by the forces of life, so that the dying earth existence can truly be re-enlivened. Every morning we can say to ourselves anew: 'I want to and I can serve the goal of re-enlivening by trying to serve Christ. I can try to seek the spiritual on earth and strive for its realization as well as I am able. With devotion I can participate in and support the sacraments with the consciousness that, through them, the re-enlivening power of Christ streams into the earth in a particular way.'

So we can, perhaps, sum up the fundamental Christian feeling of the second sentence in the words: 'For my life I can thank the Son. *Through him* I am permitted to work *with him* on the re-enlivening of the dying earth existence.'

2.3 Christ, our brother

The third sentence of the Creed reads: *In Jesus the Christ entered as man into the earthly world.* With this next powerful step the Creed leads us out of the world of all-encompassing creative powers into the region where Christ appears as man.

Certainly no part of the Christian confession has, in the past, been the cause of so many loving thoughts, so many devoted feelings of reverence, as the thought: God became one of us. Although this idea does not occur in the Apostles' Creed, still it is found in a much more detailed form in the Nicene Creed. *Homo factus est.* And so, it sounds together with the words *Et incarnatus est* in the great compositions of the Latin Mass of Beethoven, Bach, and Bruckner in a never-ending, truly moving fashion.

It has always been felt that there is an endless mystery here. In Paul's Letter to the Philippians (2:5–8) he speaks in such fashion that we cannot but notice how moved he is:

Have this mind among yourselves, which is yours in Christ Jesus, who, though he was in the form of God, did not count equality with God a thing to be grasped, but emptied himself, taking the form of a servant, being born in the likeness of men. And being found in human form he humbled himself and became obedient unto death, even death on a cross.

What does it mean that he became man? Let us imagine moments where we have really experienced genuine 'humanness', pure humanity, such as we might encounter at an unconscious stage in a small child, but also perhaps in an old person, who has 'learned' love and selflessness through a long life and has become fully mature. If we think of such complete humanity, intensified to its highest perfection, then we begin to feel a little of the pure humanity which appeared in Christ Jesus on earth and which can appear for us today.

Why are we so deeply touched? Is it not that in such a full humanity there lived a profound understanding of everything human, even all suffering and all human errors, and that this is at the same time entirely permeated, drenched even, with love?

By becoming man, Christ draws close to us in a way differing from his divine being. As God he appears to us worthy of devotion. We trust in his power. As a human being, he becomes our brother, who is close to us with an intimate humanity which understands. He lovingly understands all. Because he has become man, he can feel with us just as a human being feels joy and pain. Because the humanity of man was completely and purely fulfilled in him, he can unite the deepest compassion and understanding with pure love.

The divinity of God does not appear in Christ anthropomorphized, as it can be seen in the Greek gods, who on the one hand had superearthly abilities, but on the other, proved to be all too human. Christ has not merely been clothed in a human form, rather he became human in the highest sense possible, in the sense of pure humanness. If we want to imagine a picture of Christ we can imagine him as truly human, humanely close. We are permitted to fashion a picture of him as ideally human but with an intimate heartfelt closeness to us; with love for every single, individual human being; with the deepest understanding of everything which is human, human suffering and need, human destiny; with all human striving and happiness encompassed by his understanding. Awareness of this can give us immediate comfort and help through the day.

Again we can look at the destinies of people, who in their lives, were permitted to experience this divine human closeness of Christ. For example, Gabriele Bossis, (1874–1950), a prolific Catholic writer, whose diary gives us a wonderful witness to the path she was permitted to walk often in the most difficult situations of her destiny. She was able to experience the nearness of Christ as an inner voice:

You are never alone. This certainty should be a
strong source of strength for you. It gives you
the courage to speak to me because I am there.
Courage to act because I can help you,
especially when you speak with others.
   ... I am the one who created human nature. I
know about its weaknesses, its lowliness. Do
not be amazed, however, that I still love you.
No, do not be amazed. I lived among you.
   ... Consider my love ... what is yours, is in
the deepest existence of your being mine ...
Think about it: I am closer to you than you are
to yourself.
   ... Believe me, I am never far from you.
   ... Think upon this, even if I am entirely God,
so also I am, at the same time, entirely human.
   ... Even if I do not speak with you, that does
not mean that I am far from you. I am present.

I am dedicated to every soul as if it were the only one in the world.

And that is what can grow out of the third sentence of the Creed for us: To feel the Christ very close, close as one person is to another; to think of and feel Christ as the one who understands; and who out of understanding loves; and out of love he is the God who comforts; as the brother of man who accompanies our life with an endless closeness.

2.4 The birth of Christ in the soul

The fourth sentence of the Creed reads: *The birth of Jesus upon earth is a working of the Holy Spirit who, to heal spiritually the sickness of sin of the bodily nature of mankind, prepared the son of Mary to be the vehicle of the Christ.* The Creed moves from the working of the Father and the Son to the working of the Spirit. We stand before one of the fundamental statements of Christianity. What does Holy Spirit mean?

We have looked at the Father as the one who subsists or stands beneath or behind all being. The Son appears to us as the center of all creative life and we found these two divine realms of working summed up in the formulation 'The Father God be in us, the Son God create in us . . .' In what realm can the working of the Holy Spirit become visible to us?

When we look at the world we experience its being and its becoming, the life which fills it. There is, however, not only being and life in the world, but also order and meaning which points to a goal. Here we meet the working of the Spirit. From the Spirit comes the order found in the contours of the world. This we can behold in everything surrounding us in the world of space. From him also originates all of the meaningful development which we experience in time.

We realize how little modern natural science likes to speak of meaningful ordering in nature, of the meaning found in chronological sequences or in the development

53

of nature and history. Of course, science *has* discovered and speaks of order in the three kingdoms of nature, in groupings and reciprocal dependencies (for minerals, in the categories of crystal systems, for plants and animals, in the connections to be found between the various species, families, and so on. But all of this is supposed to be based on an accidental 'natural development' and on 'natural selection through survival of the fittest.' Even development toward higher species in the chronological appearance of life-forms from the simplest creatures all the way up to the human being is in the final analysis supposed to be accidental. In any case, this philosophy doesn't believe that the kingdoms of nature are developing toward a meaningful goal. According to this view the history of mankind, conceived in the narrowest sense, merely reveals a sequence of accidents which only appear to develop in a certain direction because man's intelligence reads a meaning into those accidents.

Modern knowledge of the spirit, however, can show in nature, as well as in the march of history, order and meaning. Here we refer the reader to the numerous results of research in which a meaningful arrangement of the cosmos is portrayed in great detail.

Truly observant common sense can immediately perceive that a rose with its perfected form, or a robin redbreast with its meaningful bodily shape and simple beauty, cannot be simply a product of accident or of the battle for the survival of the fittest. In the future, this certainty will, no doubt, receive a scientific justification.

When we direct our attention to the order and meaning of existence we see the working of the Spirit in the world. He is the one who shapes and orders the being of the Father and the creating of the Son, which he fashions in all details so that we can experience beauty and order as a mirror of the Spirit who works into all the world.

There is an order of a higher kind which is manifested in the sequence of events in human biography. Already the fact that in many destinies it is easy to find a seven-year rhythm of major events, points to such an order. But above and beyond this, a completed human life can often appear like a work of art in which the details dovetail to a large extent into a larger whole. See for example, Diether Lauenstein's book *Biblical Rhythms in Biography*. Yet, it is also clear, when one looks at many human destinies, that every one is entirely individual, unique in its kind and quality. What is it that touches us so when we hear the biographies of human beings? Just this: the irreplacable uniqueness of every single human existence on earth.

In these facts the power of the Spirit works into our lives. Certainly this should not mislead us to the view that, from the beginning to end our lives are completely determined and set through an inexorable destiny. This is not the case. The greatness of a human biography consists in this: that despite all the human errors and mistakes, a great picture can emerge. Just as a musical genius is able to dissolve all disharmonious notes and bring them into a higher unity in a work of art, so also is the Spirit which works into our destiny able to take much of that which was perhaps not intended and use it to redeem, heal, sometimes even to sanctify.

This would be much more readily perceptible if we were able to view a human destiny not only within the limits of one earthly existence but also in a sequence of earth lives. Then the riddles which can be found in every human destiny could be resolved into a much greater picture. Not only would they then be able to appear in a much higher ordering, but above all, they could be seen with their meaning. Even destinies which within the limits of one earth life appear to be completely wasted, for example, of criminals or mentally or physically handicapped people, find an inner justification and balance when seen in connection with the previous or the next life.

In looking at the work of the Spirit in this way we turn again to the fourth sentence of the Creed. There the birth of Jesus is described as a working of the Holy Spirit: '... who ... prepared the son of Mary to be the vehicle of the Christ.' Here it must be expressly stressed that this statement in no way intends to renew the old dogma concerning the virgin birth of Jesus through Mary. This dogma is, with respect to the bodily conditions, a misunderstanding of facts which belong on the spiritual plane. The conception and birth of the boy Jesus was an entirely proper development.

The text of this sentence in the Apostles' Creed reads as follows: 'Conceived by the Holy Ghost, born of the Virgin Mary.' We see how the new Creed avoids the easily misunderstood text, yet nevertheless, expresses the working of the Holy Spirit. How is this to be understood?

A key to the answer is offered in the New Testament where the long list of ancestors of Jesus is recounted (Matthew 1 and Luke 3). In the order seen there nothing is accidental. The descent is traced from Adam through Abraham and all the way down through the generations. The birth of Jesus was prepared by the Spirit's power to give order, create meaning and set goals. The heredity and the processes which build the body were guided so that the proper vehicle for the indwelling of the divine Son in a human being could be offered in the bodily nature of Jesus.

Here we can see the mystery of the working of the Spirit as it guides earthly processes and destinies through the centuries so that they become transparent and receptive for spiritual content. Precisely this kind of spiritual penetration of the earthly stands behind the secret of the so-called virgin birth. In Mary's devotion to the spiritual processes associated with the conception and birth, of the approach of a human soul who through the working of the Holy Spirit was destined to receive the Christ, that all of the earthly activities connected with it did not appear in her consciousness at all. All earthly desire was absent, and so the soul, the spirit of Mary, could remain pure and virginal, untouched by earthly darkness. She was lifted out of herself. In this way the soul which was to enter the earth through this birth could remain pure. Its spiritual source could unite with the bodily nature in a less darkened way than would have otherwise been the case.

Thus, Jesus could become the vehicle of the Christ. The earthly hereditary line was prepared through the centuries so that his body and soul nature could be pure and transparent enough to be molded into a vessel for the divine, to produce an earthly body capable of being so spiritualized that it could resurrect as a spiritual body. (To read further about the mystery of the Resurrection, see Emil Bock's book *The Three Years* or Friedrich Benesch's book *Easter*.)

In this way through the indwelling of Christ in an earthly body it was for the first time, possible for 'the sickness of sin of the bodily nature of mankind' to be healed. The effects of error, sickness and death were overcome in a human body and lifted away.

The Creed points to this mystery by stressing the part played by the Spirit who, 'to heal *spiritually* the sickness of sin of the bodily nature of mankind . . .'

What can all of this mean for my own life? Are not all of these facts far removed from what would affect me?

Christianity has always known about the mystery of Mary in the human soul. In Mary something like an archetype of the best human soul forces emerges. Angelus Silesius summed this up in the words: 'If Christ is born a thousand times in Bethlehem and not in you, you remain eternally lost.' It becomes clear what our part in the truth of the fourth sentence of the Creed can be. In our soul also there is a Mary mystery. The mystery of a higher birth works in us and the power of the Holy Spirit can be found in our lives also. The very fact that we may now stand at a turning in our lives where we are receptive for spiritual questions, depends on the angelic guidance of destiny, a guidance which we have perhaps experienced for a long time. We can know we are united with the working of the Spirit through the wisdom underlying our destiny. We can trust that all of our experiences are related to a goal and have meaning.

But life also brings us challenges and responsibilities. The fact that we are led to an openness to the Spirit also presents us with the duty to activate receptiveness for spiritual truths. Or precisely, in the words of the Creed, to build 'a vehicle for the Christ.' To allow him to be born in us.

With this we return to a motif of the second sentence. Now, however, it appears to us in a much more intimate form. There we spoke of uniting with the re-enlivening power of Christ and through our actions carrying it into the world to strengthen its working there. Here we see the possibility of transforming our own soul forces to permit the Christ to work in us and through us. The question can move our hearts. How can we form and change our thinking, our feeling and our doing so that Christ can live within them. We prepare here for what will appear again in the eleventh sentence in a higher connection: To 'feel the Christ within themselves . . . who are aware of the health-bringing power of the Christ.'

In the ritual of The Christian Community the motif of 'Christ in me' is central. At the end of an earth life this is raised to a higher level and intensified. The funeral service speaks of 'soul deeds', of feeling Christ in the soul and taking him up into thought. At the conclusion we are reminded that we are beholden to the Spirit for all our thoughts, words and deeds.

Such thoughts can move us in our hearts when, at the beginning of the day, we use the fourth sentence of the Creed. We attempt to bring to mind that we have been led by the Spirit thus far in our destiny so that the will to serve the Christ can awaken in us. Gratitude fills us. We may also look with thankfulness at the fact that we can gradually transform the forces in our soul to become a vehicle, a 'raiment' for the Christ. We can bear in mind too, that the power of Mary also dwells in our soul and we shall perhaps consider how to shape thoughts, feelings, words and actions in the critical moments of the day so that Christ can live within them, so that he is born not only in us but also into the world?

We must admit that we are only able to achieve this

in small measure. It is not the intention here to recommend any sentimental moods of the soul which are estranged from the world. However, if we are always able to admit our failings, then the moments will increase in which in an honest and healthy way, we can sense and achieve something of the deepest goals of mankind.

The Acts of the Apostles (11:26) describes how in Antioch quite some time after the life of Christ the name 'Christian' appeared. The name 'Christian' is ascribed to those who confess him, who have taken him into their hearts. Are we permitted seriously to bear his name? Perhaps we are, if more and more we struggle to allow him to live in us.

The following fundamental mood of soul can arise from the fourth sentence of the Creed: With gratitude I can look upon the guidance of the Spirit in my life. He prepares me for the task of giving space for Christ in me, a vehicle for Christ in the world.

The first and highest birth which took place
before all time is that the heavenly Father bore
his only Son in divine existence. The second birth
was in time. It is the maternal birth in
Bethlehem, which occurred in virginal modesty
and in proper purity. The third birth is not
bound to any time, it is above all time: a God is
truly spiritually born in every soul in every day
and at all hours with grace and with love.

(From a Christmas Sermon by Johannes Tauler)

2.5　The suffering of Christ

The fifth sentence of the Creed reads: *The Christ Jesus suffered under Pontius Pilate the death on the cross and was lowered into the grave of the earth.* This sentence is understandable from events described in the Gospel. We can, therefore, go directly to the question: What does it say to us?

With the fourth sentence we tried to make clear how we are able to do something for the divine in the world. Now, however, comes the other side. There is also a working against the Spirit and we would not be honest if we did not admit that we also participate in this. The figure of Pontius Pilate stands as a representative for every human being just as Mary represented for the positive force which can be found in every human soul. In the picture of Mary we acquired a feeling for that in us which is capable of being Christian. Now we must also look at that in us which stands *against* the divine. The phrase 'under Pontius Pilate' points beyond the figure of Pilate himself to all that occurred under his authority: which the betrayal, the error, the mockery, the brutality, the denial and weakness.

The fifth sentence points us to earnest self-knowledge. That which in us leads to the suffering of the divine, can be looked at, must be deeply felt. This sentence should not only remind us of a historical fact; through it something above time and ever-present is expressed as part of the Christian Creed. Here the words concerning the 'Lamb of God, who takes away the sin of the world' (John 1:29) become acutely present and stir those feelings which connect us with Christ in a very powerful way. The openness to the Spirit which arose in us through experience with the fourth sentence is deepened through the perception of our error and weakness. When we are forced to feel how strongly the forces against the divine work within us, our wills are strengthened for 'Christ in us.'

We see here how the fourth and fifth sentences belong together and complete one another. If the fourth sentence leads us to a one-sided Mary mood, then the fifth sets us back on the hard ground of fact which we are not permitted to overlook if our religious life is not to become superficial and unhealthy. If, on the other hand, the content of the fifth sentence oppresses us excessively, then the fourth, with its positive view of the forces in our soul, can be a comfort. It works as a counterweight against any one-sided consciousness of sin.

There is yet something else contained in the fifth sentence which can touch our hearts directly. It has always been felt and understood that Christ suffered and died for every human being. This feeling has been summed up in the words *'pro nobis'*, which means, 'for us.' There is much truth in this feeling; today, two thousand years after the crucifixion, we can still feel that if this death had not been experienced, this pain not suffered, then Christ would not be able to be present in *our* death and *our* suffering. Through the fact that he suffered and died he has united himself with all suffering and all death in the world. He is not a God who hovers above the world and from a divine distance, views and judges mankind. Rather he has descended all the way

into the depths of human exist nce in order to fill the
depths and the abysses w   fe. Through the deed
of the cross long ag   of the divine was
implanted in man's   God and today
reaffirms itself in every   of human need
and suffering.

Christ suffers within o   else can we
understand the words 'as   of the least
of these my brethren, you   att.25:40).
And from this point of view   incredible
suffering which has been given   can see
the painful question of many   God
allow this? We can really come to   and
love of God when we see others su.   aps
when we suffer ourselves.

But things look different if we bear in mind
happens to any one also happens to Christ, that i.
suffering he suffers too. Why? Because in every hour o
suffering he wants to plant a seed for its overcoming.

Why doesn't he simply take the pain away from
mankind? What if it is the pain of a higher birth? Is
there anything great in the world without the pain of
birth? Can the greatest thing in the world, the conscious
personal relationship of the human self to God come
into existence without this pain? In the farewell
discourse of St John's Gospel there are words of Christ
which point to this mystery of birth. When Christ leaves
the disciples he gives them words of comfort:

> Truly, truly, I say to you, you will weep and
> lament, but the world will rejoice; you will be
> sorrowful, but your sorrow will turn into joy.
> When a woman is in travail she has sorrow,
> because her hour has come; but when she is
> delivered of the child, she no longer remembers

the anguish, for joy that a child is born into the
world. So you have sorrow now, but I will see
you again and your hearts will rejoice, and no
one will take your joy from you.' (John
16:20–22).

Our suffering has a meaning. The Christ did not say:
'You suffer the pain and I'll watch.' He is in our pain
and overcomes it. Some day we shall be able to recognize this. We can become more and more conscious of
his overcoming the pain and learn from him at least to
bear up better under our suffering and then, eventually,
to overcome it ourselves. '*Pro nobis*', for us, truly he
does this for us, so that we, one day *with him* and
through him will also be able to overcome.

There is yet another step we can take. A poem by
Conrad Ferdinand Meyer, 'Die Krypte' describes how in
every old church, no matter how majestic it may be, no
matter how far it may ascend into the heights and into
the light, still has a crypt.

> Forget not the crypt! That is where the holy head
> which bore the sharp thorns wound around must
>   be turned.
> I believe some will climb down there below,
> several will feel comfort.
> We may, when suffering surrounds us like night,
> behold then, not happiness nor fame, only greater
>   pain.

With this feeling we can also unite with something
which was more alive in the past of Christianity when
a man could see through his own pain, his own
suffering, to the greater pain of Christ, who was united

with the Cross. Through this he could feel comfort for his own existence.

So in the fifth sentence of the Creed we find several different directions developed in a very significant way. I am deeply united with Christ through the fact that he has taken my mistakes, my guilt into himself. He is united with me in the deepest way possible because he suffers my suffering, and into my suffering and into my death pours his life even if I do not notice it. I am permitted to feel comfort for my own destiny when I look upon the destiny of the Cross on which Christ suffered.

2.6 Above and beyond death

The sixth sentence of the Creed reads: *In death he became the helper of the souls of the dead who had lost their divine nature*. These words point to a deed of Christ which requires special discussion. In the New Testament there is only a hint concerning it. For example, '[Christ] went and preached to the spirits in prison, who formerly did not obey' (1Pet.3:19f). We find further hints in Paul's Letter to the Ephesians (4:9), 'In saying, "He ascended," what does it mean but that he had also descended into the lower parts of the earth?' Also in his Letter to the Romans (14:9), 'For to this end Christ died and lived again, that he might be Lord both of the dead and of the living.'

What is being expressed here? We are directed to a secret, mysterious event which Christ performed when he entered the realm of the dead. After the death on the cross his body rested in the grave of the earth, but he himself now entered into a region on the other side of the threshold of death, not as a man subject to death, that is, not as a man overcome by death, who has been robbed of his power, but rather in the fullness of his divine human authority.

It is like a sunrise for the souls who 'had lost their divine nature.' The first rays of the resurrection light show before Easter morning in the realm of the dead. It would seem, then, that the power of death had been broken. The consequences of this event rayed forth and affected all souls which, in pre-Christian times, had united so deeply with material existence that, after death they could no longer awaken themselves.

We have in Homer's *Odyssey* (book II), a painful description of how the early Greeks (around the eighth century BC) experienced and regarded death. Odysseus manages to find the path into the realm of the dead, Hades. He encounters the dead there as dark shadows groaning and hopelessly grieving for their past earth lives. The description becomes even darker and more hopeless when he enters the region where the deeds of the previous earth lives must find penance. He experiences Sisyphus and Tantalus, the eternal senseless torture.

Pre-Christian mankind became aware of the terrors of the kingdom of the dead in such pictures. Modern science of the spirit confirms that the darkening of the soul after death in the time before Christ had already reached an incredible proportion without any hope for this condition to be lighted.

Christ broke down the doors to this kingdom of the adversary powers. He penetrated into a world where for many souls the spirit could no longer shine. He became the 'helper of the souls of the dead who had lost their divine nature.'

Although the Gospels themselves do not give any description of this event, we have another witness which comes from the past and gives us, in impressive pictures, a report, the so-called Gospel of Nicodemus, an apocryphal writing of early Christianity which was not taken up into the New Testament.

The report given by the Gospel of Nicodemus of the events surrounding Christ's descent was transformed into drama in the Middle Ages as the *Redentin Easter Play*.

But the content of the sixth sentence also appears in

the Apostles' Creed. There it says that Christ 'descended into hell' — another example of how the old forms indeed express what is true but in a way that is hardly understandable for today's human being. Then too, the word 'hell' for us today implies also the descent of Christ *ad infernos*, to 'the below', as is literally stated in the Latin text.

We can see in early Christianity the mighty transformation brought about by Christ's deed in the realm of the dead. The resignation of the Greek age has disappeared. In the attitude of the martyrs it becomes clear that the fear of death was overcome. The anniversary of the day upon which someone died was celebrated as his birthday in the spirit. The nearness of the dead was experienced with the nearness of the Christ.

This sixth sentence of the Creed can open for us a relationship to those who have gone before us. We suffer again and again from the illusion that they are separated from us. But when we strive to live a spiritual life they are close to us.

The Act of Consecration of Man can teach us about this. Three times those who have passed over the threshold are brought into the service. At the beginning of the Offering where the dead are called upon to offer the sacrifice along with those present. At the beginning of the Transubstantiation (the third part of the Act of Consecration of Man) where those are addressed who have gone ahead and have brought Christ to life within them for they can be close to us with their protective power. And at the end of the Transubstantiation where all those are borne in mind who before us have already brought the Christ-offering.

A Christianity of the present and future needs knowledge concerning the realm of the dead. Above all because today they need our help. Every soul who crosses the threshold of death in this present age has an immense burden of darkness within. This load, the result of the darkened aspects of our age will make the path after death endlessly difficult. The dead need our thoughts. Thoughts which come with the light of Christ can offer help today. Long ago Christ made the way clear through which help could come into the kingdom of the dead. Today he needs the help of human beings. Through us he can shine light into the darkness of death.

That awareness is what this sentence of the Creed can stimulate in our consciousness and in our feelings: Through Christ there is a bridge over the abyss of death. Through the power of Christ the dead want to live with us. Death does not have a final decisive power and it loses its terror. At the same time, however, our connections to the dead become an admonition for us: In the words of Goethe, 'They call from beyond, the voices of spirits, the voices of the masters, forget not to practise the strength of the good. We tell you to hope.'

2.7 Death, the seed of a higher life

It is certainly no accident that just the seventh sentence of the Creed expresses Christianity's mystery of Resurrection and Easter: *Then he overcame death after three days.*

This sentence has a similar fundamental significance for our relationship to Christ as the first sentence has for our relationship to the Father. For here we are at the actual center of Christ's working which is connected with the overcoming of death in man and in the world.

In many ways death reaches into our human existence. It does not first meet us at the end of life. In manifold experiences and moods it is present in our daily life. When we reach the borders of our own possibilities, when we no longer know what to do next, when we have come up against exhaustion and inner powerlessness. It lives in despair and in the absolute emptiness of our inner life. There death comes to meet us. Indeed, not in bodily form but directly within the soul and spiritual part of us.

Human existence has the forces of death within it. Again and again something in us dies. We come upon death's presence in an inner way, long before we die outwardly. Many people today must constantly endure moments, days, weeks and sometimes months of suffering where they are taken hold of by an inner emptiness, feel hollowed out, and even the best thoughts and religious forces which have otherwise carried no longer help. There are moments when no prayer, no religious service, when no word from another human being can support or comfort us.

Let it again be said: such moods of soul can be intensified to the point where nothing can help. The forces of death have completely taken our soul into its possession. Yet such moments are profoundly significant for they can bring about something within us which in no other way can be awakened.

Let us look back on the path which the Creed has taken us with respect to our relationship to Christ. The second sentence helps us to become aware that life flows from Christ into the death of the world and re-enlivens what is dying and that we can participate in this. From the fourth sentence we receive word that our soul forces can be transformed into a vessel for the Christ. When this happens we enter into a deeper relationship with Christ.

Now, however, we enter into the true center of all life with Christ. For how could we have part in the overcoming of death if we ourselves have not experienced it and been, for periods of time, completely under its power. At such moments something entirely new is created in the soul. Organs of perception are created which one day will be able to perceive the life that is stronger than death. Forces are created with which we shall be able to go beyond death.

Why are we in such black moments so completely helpless and lost? Because our usual everyday life fills our consciousness and supports us and then we have no reason to create eyes for the higher life which is so close to us. We do not yet see or feel it. But these experiences of powerlessness build something in the soul; the pain has a secret creative might.

Such experiences of death become a seed of higher life

within. A human being like Paul could speak of them. For again and again, indeed every day, he encountered death and through this experience was awakened to a higher life. There are many places in his letters which witness to this death-life experience.

> We are . . . always carrying in the body the death
> of Jesus, so that the life of Jesus may also be
> manifested in our bodies. For while we live we
> are always being given up to death for Jesus'
> sake, so that the life of Jesus may be manifested
> in our mortal flesh. So death is at work in us,
> but life in you. (2Cor.4:9–12)

In the experiences which Paul here describes there are further perspectives which we can only begin to understand today. For what is meant in the seventh sentence of the Creed by 'the overcoming of death' is related to all of human existence, including the body. We have been speaking up to now of experiences in the soul.

It was possible for the Christians to experience the power of 'death's overcoming' all the way into the body. Paul was able to experience the overcoming of bodily weaknesses and could bear up under unbelievable physical bodily burdens because of his relationship to Christ. For us it is perhaps only possible to acquire a feeling for the wonder of such experiences. Yet, even today all the strength to bear up and the effort to overcome which we are able to bring forth works in a transforming way, gently transmuting our bodily nature. This can be perceived in the face of a human being where the spirit can in part be read as if it were written. Often it becomes visible in the facial characteristics of one who has died. It can be startling at times to see that which appears briefly as the imprint of the spiritual in the body.

There is no doubt that gentle forces of spiritualization reach all the way into our bodily nature. These forces will become stronger. They will grow precisely through our experiences of death. We can see this indicated in many destinies of the present time where in the most extreme life-threatening situations a kind of break-through to higher forces of life was experienced. These forces of life were felt all the way into the body.

Representative of much that we are here discussing is the destiny of Jacques Lusseyran who, lying deathly ill in the concentration camp in Buchenwald, was given up as near death.

> I knew exactly what it was, this thing I was watching: my body in the act of leaving this world, not wanting to leave it right away, not even wanting to leave it at all. I could tell by the pain my body was causing me, twisting and turning in every direction like snakes that have been cut in pieces.
>
> Have I said that death was already there? If I have I was wrong. Sickness and pain, yes, but not death. Quite the opposite, life, and that was the unbelievable thing that had taken possession of me. I had never lived so fully before.
>
> Life had become a substance within me. It broke into my cage, pushed by a force a thousand times stronger than I. It was certainly not made of flesh and blood, not even of ideas. It came towards me like a shimmering wave, like the caress of light. I could see it beyond my eyes and my forehead and above my head. It touched me and filled me to overflowing. I let myself float upon it.
>
> There were names which I mumbled from the

depths of my astonishment. No doubt my lips
did not speak them, but they had their own song:
'Providence, the Guardian Angel, Jesus Christ,
God.' I didn't try to turn it over in my mind. It
was not just the time for metaphysics. I drew
my strength from the spring. I kept on drinking
and drinking still more. I was not going to leave
that celestial stream. For that matter it was not
strange to me, having come to me right after my
old accident when I found I was blind. Here was
the same thing all over again, the Life which
sustained the life in me.

The Lord took pity on the poor mortal who
was so helpless before him. It is true I was quite
unable to help myself. All of us are incapable of
helping ourselves. Now I knew it, and knew
that it was true of the SS among the first. That
was something to make one smile.

But there was one thing left which I could do:
not refuse God's help, the breath he was
blowing upon me. That was the one battle I had
to fight, hard and wonderful all at once: not to
let my body be taken by the fear. For fear kills,
and joy maintains life.

Slowly I came back from the dead, and when,
one morning, one of my neighbours — I found
out later he was an atheist and thought he was
doing the right thing — shouted in my ear that
I didn't have a chance in the world of getting
through it, so I had better prepare myself, he
got my answer full in the face, a burst of
laughter. He didn't understand that laugh, but
he never forgot it.*

* And there was Light, reprinted by Floris Books, Edinburgh 1985, pp. 221f.

Lusseyran then describes how some of this 'life within death' flowed from him to the other prisoners and how he was able to help them in their misery. 'I could turn towards them the flow of light and joy which had grown so abundant in me ... Almost everyone forgot I was a student ... For many, I was just "the man who didn't die".'

We can witness here a proclamation of the power of resurrection that reaches all the way into the bodily nature.

Such experiences are fundamental to Christianity. They can appear subtly in the life of every man. Decisive experiences such as Lusseyran's will increase. This belongs to the future destiny of mankind.

Much of what we have been describing can be used as content for our morning observations when we turn to the seventh sentence of the Creed. These observations will prepare us for those moments when death is at work in our soul. Perhaps they will not be able to help us directly with immediate problems. However, they can be like a ray of hope which in the not too distant future, can be like a shining light in the darkness of our souls.

In this darkness we shall be able to say to ourselves: What I now experience is not the last word. Even this death which I am now suffering has already in its innermost being been overcome by Christ, for he overcame all death. The deepest meaning of our work with the Creed is this: That for the darkest hours of our life, if not immediate help, at least real hope will come to us.

2.8 The Lord of the heavenly forces upon earth

The eighth sentence of the Creed reads: *Since that time he is the Lord of the heavenly forces upon earth and lives as the fulfiller of the fatherly deeds of the ground of the world.*

With the eighth sentence we move to the second part of the Creed. The first sentences are concerned with the deeds of the Christ from the past. (More precisely the third through the seventh are in the past tense, 'he did', 'he suffered', and so on.) We have attempted to show how those deeds work and create the foundation for our Christian existence today.

The facts working from the past are transformed into events of the present and the future. The eighth sentence of the Creed lives entirely in the present, 'he is', 'he lives', although it is still connected with a historical event of Christ's working on earth, with his Ascension.

What do the words 'heavenly forces upon earth' mean? Much can come to mind if we ask, where do we experience such heavenly forces? In nature they meet us with an incredible fullness and beauty. There would be no life on earth if the sun, or indeed, the entire heaven with planets and stars did not make this life possible. In the beauty and fullness of life in nature we have a reflection of the heavenly forces which work on earth.

But all of this would not exist today, would no longer

exist were it not for the Christ. We remember the statements made concerning the second sentence of the Creed when we spoke about the re-enlivening of the dying earth existence. Today, we would be standing before the grave of the earth if Christ had not united his life with it and in that way saved it and renewed it. He is thus mysteriously connected with all life. Novalis knew about this. 'He is the star, he is the sun, he is the source of eternal life. From plant and stone and sea and light shines his childlike countenance.'

Art is another realm in which we are able to experience the heavenly forces upon earth. Perhaps not everything today called art arises from the working of such forces. But the great works of art of the past and present are great for precisely this reason: they transfigure the earthly in some way. That means they unite earthly forces with heavenly forces. We can recognize Christ as the guide and bestower, as the lord of these forces.

But is everything then said? Certainly not. For now our glance turns to the great sphere of human existence itself. Every child can still ray into our lives pure and unsullied heavenly forces which it brings with it from the preearthly. But also later on, in the great and small moments of life, our destiny can be surrounded and enveloped by the forces of a higher world, whose lord we recognize and worship as the Christ. We mention here, moments of pure love, pure devotion, of the joy of overcoming and of consolation, of light-filled knowledge, of prayer and meditation, and finally, the influence of spiritual and religious life. In the Sacraments in particular there is a stream of heavenly forces upon earth.

We can bear in mind that we are constantly in touch

with these that our life, even when it appears to be poor and dark, nevertheless is rich, if only we are awake to the small and great wonders which we encounter every day.

> How much beauty there is on earth invisibly
>   strewn,
> I would like more and more to become aware of.
> How much beauty which shies away from the noise
> of the day in quiet modest hearts of both old and
>   young.
> Be it only the fragrance of flowers, still it
> makes the loveliness of the meadow a smile among
>   much pain.
>
> (Christian Morgenstern)

If we can live our days bearing this in mind then we become aware how the heavenly forces penetrate the world and our destiny. We become grateful for all that we can experience in this way.

And this thankfulness finally turns to Christ himself. With joy we receive what, in the final analysis, he as the Lord of these forces bestows upon us. Through this we become united with the Christ in a totally new way.

If we think back on the various ways of relating to Christ which have, up to this point, been stimulated by the Creed, it becomes clear that our relationship is different now. We are permitted not only to experience him through pain and suffering and in the transformation of our own souls, but also in joy over great and beautiful things, in our joy at the richness and majesty of existence. When we have understood and deeply felt that the pain of life is there to awaken us to a higher side of life, only then are we able not to misuse the joys of existence in a one-sided illusionary way. Then we are permitted to receive them out of the hands of Christ.

The Gospel is interwoven with the sound of joy. At the birth announcement of the angel we hear the words: 'I bring you good news of a great joy which will come to all the people' (Luke 2:10). And further on again: 'Rejoice!' The Christianity cultivated in the East has been able to preserve this note even to the present time. In the Easter greeting of the Russian Church it can still be heard. The overcoming of death in the world is the reason for this great joy. All other joys would be in vain, must ultimately end in a great sadness if death had not been defeated.

Since this has happened, however, we are permitted in other moments of life to be sincerely joyous because we know that our joy is taken up into the 'great joy'.

From all that has been said it is clear that the old picture of the Ascension, in which Christ *distances* himself from the earth, requires a correction. Ascension signifies an elevation over the earth, above the earth, a freeing from its attachments: no longer attached to any one place or time in a bodily shape, it is thus we find Christ. With an exalted power, the power of the heavenly forces, he shows himself to be present on earth living and creating a connection between heaven and earth.

So he becomes 'the fulfiller of the fatherly deeds of the ground of the world.' With this second part of the eighth sentence, our attention is guided from receiving the joys of existence to active cooperation and working with Christ. For when we unite ourselves with Christ we are able to be involved with his work carrying out the intentions of the ground of the world. We can participate very little in the work of the heavenly forces in the realms of nature. In the practice of art, it is possible to do more. But above all it is in our own lives and in spiritual and religious activities that we can consciously join in the work of Christ.

The eighth sentence of the Creed leads us to joy and gratitude for what we can daily experience in the small and great wonders in the kingdoms of the world. We learn not to experience any day without this gratitude. But above and beyond this, we are called to participate actively in the work of Christ. Every Act of Consecration, every prayer, every word of the Gospel contains heavenly forces offered to man and through which men can work into the realm of the earthly. We find that in response to our gratitude we feel a sense of responsibility for these forces bestowed upon us. However, they must be carried in the right way. Uniting with Christ we share in the divine actions which bring the world forward. This sentence of the Creed especially can help us daily to become co-workers of God upon earth. It relates us to both the future and the present.

As a fundamental state of mind or mood, we find in the eighth sentence the following: I thank Christ for the small and great joys of my life. I am permitted to participate in the divine deeds which bring the world forward, whose fulfiller is the Christ.

2.9 The advancement of the world

The ninth sentence reads: *He will in time unite for the advancement of the world with those whom, through their bearing, he can wrest from the death of matter.* In this sentence we hear both triumph and tragedy. 'The advancement of the world.' There will be an advance! But then come the words concerning the 'death of matter' and the possibility appears that the souls of men could become the prey of this death, and might not be wrested free from it.

We encounter here for the first time the motif which at the end of the Creed will awaken great earnestness in us: that the working of Christ in the future is connected with the behavior of human beings; that a happy ending to the events of world history is not guaranteed. Here lies tribute to the freedom of mankind. The Godhead would not be taking mankind seriously if he did not hold man responsible for the consequences of his actions.

In earlier times of Christianity there was something deeply terrifying about the idea that eternal damnation was possible from the results of one human lifetime. We understand that the intention was to raise the serious-ness of decisions made in this one earth life. It is not our intention to detract from that, as we now point to the ancient wisdom of reincarnation renewed through modern science of the spirit. Man can fulfill his destiny only in more than one earth life.* Everything is not lost

* See, for example, Rudolf Frieling's book *Christianity and Reincarnation*.

in one life on earth. A destiny which appears today abysmal and hopeless may in a next life experience a decisive turn, though, perhaps only with great pain.

This view of the possibility of a future 'balancing out' should, however, not take anything away from the decisive earnestness of every human life. For what is neglected today must be caught up with later and under more difficult conditions. Only with pain can it be brought back into harmony, else one day there really will be a 'too late'.

Knowing about future possibilities of destiny is on the one hand an infinite comfort. But it must not mislead us into *not* doing things which it is possible to do today. We must attempt to do things which perhaps can only be done today. However, whether or not a human being has a future and will live on with Christ is not decided in one lifetime alone.

The Creed speaks of a 'death of matter' but it remains open as to whether or not under all circumstances there must be human beings who fall prey to this death. The Creed does not mention any predestination of this sort. Perhaps the development of mankind, which still has great expanses of time ahead of it, will follow such a course that humanity as a whole can participate in the advancement of the world.

However, it *is* stated that it depends upon the behavior or bearing of the individual whether or not he can be taken into it. What could be meant with the word 'bearing' can be seen in much of that which we have already discussed. In the concept of 'bearing' we find a summary of all the ways of behaving, and the attitudes which unite us with Christ: to shape the soul into a vehicle of Christ — to experience his nearness in

suffering — to accept death within us as a seed of higher
life — to work with him in the sense of heavenly forces
on earth.

Men today can have many different feelings about the
future. One can sense and feel the future like a doom
coming toward us so that one is at the mercy of his
destiny. Another possible feeling is: I can, through my
attitudes, actions and bearing actively participate in
shaping my future as well as that of the world, even
only through very modest positive forces which I am
able to develop. This feeling can be enhanced to the
point where we sense that some part of the advancement
of the world cannot take place without us. Paul speaks
concerning this situation in his Letter to the Romans
(8:18–23) when he says:

> I consider that the sufferings of this present time
> are not worth comparing to the glory that is to
> be revealed to us. For the creation waits with
> eager longing for the revealing of the sons of
> God; for the creation was subjected to futility,
> not of its own will but of the will of him who
> subjected it in hope; because the creation itself
> will be set free from its bondage to decay and
> obtain the glorious liberty of the children of God.
> We know that the whole creation has been
> groaning in travail together until now; and not
> only the creation, but we ourselves, who have
> the first fruits of the Spirit groan inwardly as we
> wait for adoption as sons, the redemption of
> our bodies.

In these words we see the significance of the future of
mankind, not only for man himself but also for the
'creatures', for all creation. This, then, is 'the advancement of the world.' But does that mean only the

83

advancement of mankind, of the human world? Or are the worlds above and below the human also included? Paul points in this direction.

What comes to pass through man's 'bearing' receives then a much greater meaning. The conduct of men has consequences on a world scale. The Christ will one day seek to unite with those men who can bring him power 'for the advancement of the world.' This is at the same time the power which enables him to free men from the rigid bonds of matter, which, speaking with Paul, are the tyranny of the past. Here we can learn to feel this: 'through my conduct, my attitude, my bearing, the future arises.' The future isn't simply there. It is created out of the many events which can serve the Spirit in the world of men and as a spiritual power is at the disposal of the advancement of the world.

Without human beings capable in the future of experiencing a union with the Christ, no advance would be possible. The Creed stimulates us to consider how our actions serve advancement or perhaps work to its detriment. This objective point of view should be the source of our motivation and not the all too subjective question: Will those who are connected with me be present in the new world?

The fundamental feeling behind the ninth sentence of the Creed is: I can work for the advancement of the world. To this end, I will unite myself with Christ.

2.10 Healing through the Spirit

The tenth sentence of the Creed reads: *Through him can the healing Spirit work.* The fourth sentence gave us cause to consider the being and working of the Spirit. Now, towards the end of the Creed we are entering again into the sphere of the Spirit. The two concluding sentences belong also to the Spirit, even if that is not expressly stated.

Here we can expand and complete our earlier statements. We attempted to show how the Spirit orders and gives meaning to the world and how this activity becomes visible everywhere in nature and in human life. This shows *one* side of the Spirit's working. The other side is this: That the *spirit of man* can also recognize and know that ordering and healing is at work in the world. In this way the kingdom of the Spirit reaches into us and becomes within us the light of knowledge. 'The Spirit God, enlighten us.' But something else is united with knowledge. Knowledge makes freedom possible. For only when I have understood what my true connection with the world is, both the earthly and the spiritual, shall I be able to place myself freely in the whole. Without such knowledge all actions remain more or less unconscious and therefore unfree.

The Spirit God works in a very real way within our spiritual knowledge of the world. We are then able to say: 'When knowledge of the deeper connections of the world is given to me, I experience a ray of the light of

the Spirit God. This knowledge leads me step by step
into freedom.' For I become conscious of the fact that I
am a being who comes from a spiritual world and is
living in the earthly world. There are forces which can
transform me and lead me back to a proper relationship
to the spirit. I learn how the earthly world came forth
originally from the spiritual. It waits to be taken up into
the advancement of the world through the forces which
lie in human beings.

Another thought belongs here. It is possible for man
truly to recognize and understand his own relationship
to himself and to the world and out of such knowledge
then to begin doing good. Here lies the possibility for
the true healing of man, not in a medical, but in the all-
encompassing sense. The Spirit heals. It is at the same
time the Holy and Healing Spirit. What serves the
healing of man is holy and all that is holy works to heal.
There is also a nuance of wholeness; something is healed
when it is not broken but present in its entirety. The
Spirit leads man to knowledge of the wholeness of the
world, to the connection between the spiritual and the
earthly. It shows that life on earth has a meaning in the
world, in the earthly and in the spiritual cosmos and
that it has been given into the hands of man to bring it
to realization. Therein we finally find that which alone
can bring our relationship to the world into order. For
every healing which works in an external way is only
preliminary. It can and must be completed through
slowly learning to stand properly within all the relationships in the world, from within and consciously. Man
must find and establish the correct relationship even to
his own body. But this is only possible through
advancing knowledge, that is, through the Healing
Spirit.

Through Christ the working of the Spirit leads us to take hold of ourselves freely from within. As long as we do not know why we live and how we stand in our relationships we are always captive to our own subjectivity. Spiritual knowledge leads us to inner freedom and hence to the ability properly to take ourselves in hand and set objective goals for ourselves.

But we need the power to 'realize' our insights. This power to make real comes from Christ. Therefore, we read 'Through him can the healing Spirit *work*.' Not, 'can the Spirit enlighten us.' From knowledge to action, from the light of knowledge to the power of application — for this step we need the working of Christ in our lives.

That Son and the Spirit go hand in hand is expressed in words which earlier appeared as an essential summary: 'The Son God create in us, the Spirit God enlighten us.'

From this point of view we may once again to look back at the ninth sentence. Now the tenth sentence appears as a balancing addition which completes the serious drama of the ninth. The question of what becomes of souls which have fallen to the death of matter remains open. The words spoken directly after the ninth sentence with its tragic mood can appear like a subtle indication of a redemption and healing which we can feel to be far in the future.

What does all this mean for us? With this sentence in mind we can reconsider all that spiritual knowledge gives and our gratitude can be awakened for that which can live in us as the power of knowledge. We can bestir our will anew to strive after knowledge. Goethe said,

'Great thoughts and a pure heart. This is what we should ask for from God.'

We can indeed strive to permeate our lives with great ideas. To take into our hearts their purifying and healing power. But also, to pray for the strength to come a little bit further. To live up to such thoughts. That is what this sentence of the Creed can stimulate in us.

We can sum this up in the question: Does something healing go forth from my thinking and deeds, or is there much in my actions which must be seen as causing sickness and destruction? What can I do to bring more healing forces into the world, into the lives of those people who are united with me? For that is what Christ would bring about through the Healing Spirit.

The fundamental mood which goes forth from the tenth sentence is: I can receive knowledge from the light of the Spirit God and through Christ can begin to work. In this way healing forces, healing power arises for me and my fellow human beings.

Oh, there is only one problem, one single
problem in the world. Can man again be given
a spiritual significance, a spiritual restlessness,
have something descend upon him like dew
which is like the effects of a Gregorian Chant.
You see, one can no longer live from
refrigerators, from politics, from balances and
cross-word puzzles. One can no longer do it . . .
There is only one single problem, to again
discover that there is a life of the spirit standing
higher than reason — the only life which satisfies
man. It goes beyond the problem of the
religious life, which is only one form of it.
(Although perhaps the life of the spirit

necessarily leads to it.) And the life of the spirit begins there, where beyond its constituent parts a being is thought of as one.

(Antoine De Saint Exupery, *Letters to A General*)

2.11 Community

The eleventh sentence of the Creed reads: *Communities whose members feel the Christ within themselves may feel united in a Church to which all belong who are aware of the health-bringing power of the Christ.* Community — one of the essential words among important words of the present time. It is at the same time a high ideal and a goal achieved with difficulty. In the Creed, this word appears only at the conclusion. Much has gone on before. But the Spirit God unfolds an activity allowing the future to shine into the present and again, we are able to see a new side of the working of the Spirit, which leads us from isolation into community.

This becomes clear in the picture of the Whitsun events. The flame of the Spirit can be seen shining above each individual apostle, but only all of them together create the circle of the disciples. Each one speaks in his own way, but they all speak so that a great harmony arises. Self and society are not opposites but complement and form each other. How are we to understand this?

In earlier times it could be said with justification that the individual must suppress himself in order to serve the community. In part, up to the present, all communities functioned in this way: marriages, families, extended families, professional groups, guilds, the different nationalities and also churches. And formerly, this was justified

90

because the self was not yet so strongly developed and did not claim any special right for itself.

Even today, up to a certain age when the individual begins to stir, children feel best and thrive best within a healthy family group. Just as the self of a child best develops and is gifted with a healthy self-consciousness if it previously lived in a harmonious community, so must the self of mankind grow within a strong, healthy group under the protection of a presiding spirit.

But there comes a moment in every human life when the ties of the family are no longer experienced as a protection but as a hindering fetter and so the person must relentlessly, and with right, demand the stripping away of old connections in their previous form. In smaller and larger things we see this stage of development at work everywhere around us today. The old forms of community, of a folk, of professions, of churches, are breaking apart. Marriages and families are in large measure threatened. Every kind of community, of communal life and working together is under stress.

This need not come as a surprise since we are moving along the path of normal development, while the human being is progressing from group-consciousness to self-consciousness and individuality. We have arrived at an extremely unpleasant and critical stage of this development and no path leads back. For today, when an individual surrenders himself, it no longer creates community but at most, the 'mass man' who does not understand himself — as was painfully experienced in Germany at the time of the Third Reich (one Folk, one Reich, one Führer) or it leads to sects, to cliques, to racism and nationalism.

What should, what can happen? The self must find itself. Then it becomes once again capable of community. Anyone who allows the power of the self, the power of the ego to be expressed only in egotism, in self expression and assertiveness has not yet found himself. He projects, to use a term of psychology, the tensions which he has not yet mastered within himself on to the world around him. One who has really awakened to himself, can give to others some of his own strength. He does not need self-assertion and self-confirmation at the expense of others, but can help others to find their own selves in a proper way.

So the decisive question of all future community building is not how we can surrender ourselves, but how can we find ourselves? For the true 'I' of man is selfless. It is tolerant because it can feel the work of another self. Because it is capable of feeling its own worth, it can help to bear the burdens of other people and to bear *with* them because it knows that it is itself borne up and carried by the One who bears all human selves within himself, Christ.

'Communities whose members feel the Christ within themselves' is how we find it formulated in the Creed. The self of Paul was not extinguished in that he could say: 'Not I live but rather Christ lives within me.' (Gal.2:20). So are his words properly rendered. (The short form is 'Not I, but Christ in me.') Paul was, in the highest sense, an individuality because his own inexchangeable human being, had been transfigured, purified, and was present in purity through the fact that Christ dwelt within him. A picture can make this clear for us. Think of the color of old stained-glass church windows, for example. As long as the sky above is gray and the sun does not shine directly through the windows, the colors appear flat and without life. However, as soon as the sun emerges there shines in each window its own

92

wonderful color and we can never see enough of their differences. At the same time they create harmony in a higher unity, in their wholeness. It is the same sunlight which shines through each pane of glass, but the uniqueness of each pane receives its due precisely through the common sunshine. To find oneself, means at the same time, that Christ begins to work in the soul. As long as a person has not yet found himself, he must stand in the light. Or, he must at least borrow every possible light and color in order to brighten the darkness of his own existence. Only the true light which should come into the world and into every individual human being (John 1:9) can fill the being of man from within so that his own colors begin to shine pure and unclouded. This is the meaning of the Whitsun picture of the flames above the heads of the apostles.

It has by now become very clear that the path leads only forward. We must recognize and bear with one another through the difficulties of self-discovery and self-realization for they should lead beyond themselves to the goal which we discussed. As long as this goal has not entirely been achieved, only mutual respect, struggling for mutual understanding, bearing with and having patience with others on the path will bring us forward. This is not said to defend the enjoyment of egotism, but to recognize the development of the self with its crises as necessary.

Knowledge from the realm of the Spirit once again leads us forward. We can see that every single human 'I', every individual, originates from the fire of the divine 'I' as a spark which is infinitely valuable, unrepeatable in its uniqueness and in its eternal essence. It is a part of the eternal being of the Spirit. We shall feel that we must learn reverence for every human being. In a special and at the same time characteristic way Christ himself brings together the love of God and the love of one's fellow human beings when he summarizes all the commandments saying: 'You shall love the Lord your God with all your heart . . . and your neighbour as yourself.' (Luke 10:27).

We seek to learn to love our neighbor. That is the first thing which becomes clear to us from this light of the Spirit. Not love his mistakes, or the one-sided expressions of himself, but rather to love him for his real self.

When we remember that the Spirit also gives order and meaning in life we can understand the idea that human 'I's are ordered 'as the stars in heaven'. Not only does each one have a meaning which is an essential part of the world, but the spiritual ordering of these selves creates furthermore a harmony which we can sense as the working of the Spirit God.

Every human being has his own spiritual 'place' in the cosmos and a value which derives from this 'place'. By finding the way to ourselves we begin to move into the place allocated to no one else in the world, but to ourselves. We can cause the 'color' to lighten up which is only there for us. Other human beings have other places, other colors, but they all supplement one another.

This will be the wonder of future communities, that every man learns to speak and act out of his deepest innermost soul and all others can feel that the words are properly said. Others can say, 'that is truly said, that is done correctly even if I would have done or said otherwise.' We complete one another in a higher unity.

We see here the starry constellations of future

communities. But today something of this should already begin to make itself felt. We can only create communities and Christian communities today in this sense if we respect the self of every individual. The unique personality of every human being can experience and find strength and maturity through the life of the community. For today the community which is created in the renewed ritual is not created out of the past. It does not live in the denial and suppression of the individual 'I'. It is from the future and lives out of the Christ being who is felt in the soul. It works increasingly out of the power of the true human 'I'.

Review of the thoughts brought forward in the eleventh sentence of the Creed can perhaps suggest, in our morning meditations, the following consideration. Can I find today the love for my neighbor despite all external difficulties? I strive to look toward higher community, the community created from the Spirit. What can I do today so that I become capable of community, more capable and more prepared for Christian community?

2.12 Threefold hope for the future

The last sentence of the Creed reads: *They may hope for the overcoming of the sickness of sin, for the continuance of man's being, and for the preservation of their life destined for eternity.* The fruit of the previous statements is summarized in the words 'They may hope' — those 'who feel the Christ within', who 'feel his health-bringing power.'

This points to the essence of a hope which will not prove to be an illusion. In German, when a woman is expecting a child one says that she is in a condition of 'good hope.' This hope is good because its content is not found in any deceptive dream. It is rooted in the reality of life, although it will only find its fulfillment in the future.

All future events are prepared beforehand. Today we experience racing progress in the field of technology. An industry which wants to keep step must think and plan its development and production ten years in advance. It must produce the future, reach out and take hold of it, if it wants to have any future.

In a similar way that which is to become mankind's future must be prepared in the spiritual world. It is created out of the impulses of men and out of the spiritual world before it is sent down into the earthly world. There the future becomes the events of destiny. In as much as good forces work into humanity, they represent the 'good hope' of mankind. The impulses of the spiritual world unite with the prayers, thoughts and forces, both good and bad, of human beings. Only from the cooperation of the two spheres is the real future created.

What comes from mankind becomes more and more decisive as time passes. What human beings do in a positive sense is constantly becoming more important because the negative forces are present today 'by themselves' and they multiply by themselves.

The positive, however, only manifests when human beings consciously want it and do it. Yet it can outweigh the mighty negative when Christ works with mankind.

It is an error to believe that any kind of 'accident' could be responsible for events which determine the future of mankind in an essential way, for example, catastrophes or wars. Developments, decisive and essential to mankind's history, occur because of necessities which the spiritual beings leading humanity read in the spiritual world. Catastrophes will only come if they are necessary. The positive forces of mankind will give the tone for earth evolution as long as they are increasing; even though crises and great shocks to mankind must have their place in the plan for the world.

For the sake of the future we must be concerned to strengthen the positive spiritual forces in humanity. Of course, much must also be done for the future on the external field of events. There is also much which must perhaps be hindered or brought into other forms of expression: for example, in the area of the environment or in nuclear research.

But that only regulates and modifies forces working in the present. The future is created, shaped and decided upon in the spiritual world on the one hand through what happens spiritually in the souls of the human beings. Here lies the significance of all spiritual, and in particular, religious activity in the present and for the future.

On the other hand, the future is created out of that, which, coming forth from the spiritual world, is guided by angels and archangels who bring fresh forces and possibilities to mankind. This can bring something new and surprising, something that has never been seen before and could never have been predicted. Human souls also bring moods, attitudes, abilities, and will impulses with them from their pre-earthly existence, which then find expression on earth. Here too, man's spiritual and religious life is important. For within religion we practice 'openness', openness to the Spirit which allows us to take up the impulses from the spiritual world.

Needless to say, we are not speaking about a kind of religious life which questions the importance of earthly life and action. Religion should not prevent us from doing what is outwardly necessary. On the contrary, a religious life is the more healthy the less it makes the soul egotistical, and the more it strengthens us for action in our work, in the family and in every kind of human community. Nevertheless, a uniquely religious life has a different direction. Its task is to create through prayer, devotion and religious services, the connection between earth and heaven. In the offering and in praying it asks for a blessing for our earthly deeds. It unfolds forces which are just as important for humanity and the future and just as effective as are all external actions. The religious life daily creates our future in a real and effective way so that 'good hope' can live in us.

The hope for the future which is expressed in the Creed can only be found when we can say why we need not become victims of widespread fear and resignation.

When we know we can daily do something so that mankind can have 'good hope', we shall be able to turn to the threefold hope expressed in the Creed with the confidence that we are not falling into an illusion.

Let us now go a little bit further. In the Letter to the Hebrews (6:19f) there is a strange passage where hope appears in the picture of an anchor. 'We have this as a sure and steadfast anchor of the soul, a hope that enters into the inner shrine behind the curtain, where Jesus has gone as a forerunner on our behalf, having become a high priest forever after the order of Melchizedek.' Hope is a power in the soul which is thrown out like an anchor to unite the soul securely with the inner shrine from which salvation and healing proceed. Yes, we can say it represents the power which is able to draw the soul to this healing source. Hence Paul speaks of hope alongside of faith and love as one of the cardinal virtues of Christianity. The word virtue indicates a force which works in the soul in a positive way. 'So faith, hope, love abide, these three; but the greatest of these is love.' (1Cor.13:13). Therefore, hope is not something groundless. It rises in us out of the concrete experiences and feelings resulting from occupation with the Creed. In particular, it arises out of our relationship to Christ, who through his working creates a future for mankind. This in the final analysis, creates the true hope.

What then is the concrete content of our hope for the future in connection with the Creed? Three things are spoken of: 'The overcoming of the sickness of sin; the continuance of man's being; and the preservation of their life destined for eternity.'

Let us look at these briefly one at a time. The hope for the overcoming of the sickness of sin points to a fundamental change of our human existence. Basically, our whole life bears the imprint of the facts which separate us from God. To overcome this condition signifies the reunion of humanity with the divine in a new, higher, conscious relationship. 'It does not yet appear what we shall be.' So John formulated this view of hope toward a more perfect condition of man. (1John 3:2) The caterpillar and butterfly provide us with a picture for the complete transformation of a lower state into a higher one. Similarly the overcoming of the sickness of sin will bring forth a higher condition of mankind.

Today we can just make out the beginnings of this higher state. It is clear we are speaking here of a distant future. Modern science of the spirit teaches us that epochs have yet to pass before earth's development will have attained its goal. However, this future requires preparation. It will not come by itself. Through 'feeling Christ in the soul' this overcoming of the sickness of sin has already begun. It is not only real in the distant future. It begins already to work. 'It will be and is already.' These words represent a transformation of the formula of the fairy tales of childhood: 'Once upon a time . . . and if they haven't yet died, then they are still living today.'

It is appropriate that 'the continuance of man's being' follows after 'the overcoming of the sickness of sin'. Only if this continuance is not burdened with the errors and shortcomings of today's conditions does it have meaning to hope for it. Otherwise it would be better to wish for a radical end of everything affirming Mephisto's words to Faust: 'I am the spirit who always denies and properly so, for all that arises is worthy of complete destruction.' (*Faust I*, In the Den.)

But the essential being of man will not be destroyed. It will arise, endure, and continue conscious and active.

Thirdly, we read 'The preservation of their life destined for eternity.' Here the word 'their' appears particularly important. 'Their . . . life' not simply life in general. The uniqueness of every individual human being is not dissolved into a universal eternal spirituality. It is 'destined for eternity' — precisely with this unique stamp of *their* life.

In our exposition of the last sentence of the Creed we have found, in every part, a mood and motif which can serve as a foundation for contemplations in the morning. What is essential is this: That concrete hope be set against fear, especially fear of the future and against fatalistic resignation. We may summarize as follows. The reality of our future is always present in Christ. Through and with him we can work daily to create it. Hence we can hope that man and mankind will not remain as they are, that what is essential in humanity can endure all crises and that the genuine uniqueness of every human being, can be taken up into the being of eternity.

> The only thing which can signify doom for man is belief in that doom. For it hinders repentence. It hinders our turning about. (Martin Buber)

> In the midst of a humanity which is full of dreams of fear and questions about what is next going to happen, we would like to be a quiet band or community which knows what is coming. We know, namely, who is coming and if he comes then everything else can come too and we need not worry. (Emil Bock)

Survey

In conclusion, let us list the single stations along our way once again.

1. The feeling with respect to the Father
   - Protectedness within the Divine
2. The feelings with respect to the Son
   - I can thank Christ for my life
   - I feel him close to me in a human way
   - I can give him a dwelling in my heart
   - He takes my errors into himself
   - He suffers my own suffering
   - His power leads beyond death
   - Within my death there lives his overcoming of death
   - I thank him for the richness of life
   - He allows me to have part in the force which advances the world
3. The feelings with respect to the Spirit who is united with the working of the Son
   - He brings healing forces into my life
   - He creates community of spirit
   - He bestows 'good hope'

Conclusion

Practical hints

It is now, I hope, clear how the fundamental feelings and experiences of Christianity can become accessible to us through the Creed. In conclusion we would like to say something about individual work on the Creed giving suggestions and hints so that each one can find his own path of activity with the Creed.

We have spoken often of the 'contemplation or meditation in the morning.' Indeed the Creed is especially well-suited for morning contemplation if we want to use it for our daily actions. Meditated in the morning it has a chance to become an attitude working within our actions. A first basic suggestion would be this: The Lord's Prayer in the evening, the Creed in the morning. This does not mean, however, that the Lord's Prayer does not have a place in the morning prayer and that the Creed does not have its place in the evening contemplation of the day's events.

The Creed is not a prayer. In the direct addressing of the Divine, prayer has its own particular nuance. Devotion of the soul to God can gradually become a direct address, a speaking to God in prayer with 'thou'.

In the evening, in looking back over the day I can ask 'How much of that which I undertook to do in the course of the day with the help of the Creed in the morning have I been able to achieve?' Perhaps I shall have to admit that much has turned out otherwise than I intended. It would not be good to end the day with such a feeling of failure. All that I have not been able to achieve can be lifted up to the divine world in prayer — I place it into the hands of the powers which can compensate, harmonize and complete. The brief contemplation of the Creed is taken up and superseded through the praying of the Lord's Prayer.

In the morning it is important consciously and clearly to take up the impulses for the day. Here the Creed receives the main emphasis. Then afterwards in praying the Lord's Prayer I unite myself with the power that can give a blessing for this day that my best intentions may succeed. The time around midday, if the activities of the day permit, can also be a time of contemplation. One can take a short pause in the course of the day's events and use it for a moment to come to a quiet stillness. We can turn once again to the Creed. We can take up anew and strengthen the impulses of the morning, perhaps weakended by the many different tasks of the day. This does not take very long. Particularly if the morning impulses were strong, it suffices to give a short thought to them in order to awaken them again.

It is right to consider and read the whole text at intervals, perhaps on a quiet Sunday if one cannot attend the Act of Consecration of Man, or when the events of one's personal life require it, or on vacations. In daily exercises, however, it is perhaps better to take only one sentence for the content. This need take no more than a few moments.

It is good to remain with one sentence for few days perhaps, for a week or even a month. One can experiment and find out what is the best for individual needs.

It is possible, for example, to distribute the twelve sentences of the Creed over the twelve months of the year. It is more difficult, however, to match them with the festivals or the seasons. The formulations found in the Creed belong more to a realm above time. Actually only the fifth, sixth and seventh sentences can be obviously united with a festival season: Passiontide and Easter. Of course, the sixth sentence concerning the 'Helper of the souls of the dead' would belong with only one day, Holy Saturday.

Therefore, it is better to choose a rhythm which is independent of the festivals. For example, the suggested one sentence per month. Of course, one is still free then to take the corresponding sentence that matches a festival and use it in conjunction with the other. The following ordering of the sentences of the Creed with the festivals of the year may be suggested:

Advent	First Sentence
Christmas	Second and fourth sentences
Epiphany	Third sentence
Passiontide	Fifth and sixth sentences
Easter	Seventh sentence
Ascension	Eighth sentence
Whitsun	Tenth sentence

Perhaps in October one could then set the element of hope in the twelfth sentence over against the external dying in nature. In November, which is often dedicated to memories of the dead, the sixth sentence could be taken up. Occasionally we are inclined to undertake too much spiritual work, especially when we see the significance of regular practice and activity in this field and would like to contribute to it. It is, however, only realistic to admit that it is not good to take something

105

up which cannot be carried through. It is better to practice a little faithfully .

I believe, too, that today the Lord's Prayer belongs, is indispensible in the daily life of every human being who desires to work for the progress of the world. It is *the* daily prayer. The extent to which the Creed can also serve as a constant stimulation and help for our development as Christians has, I hope, become clear through this book. Anyone already accustomed to meditating on other verses in the morning, may, for fear of overextension, hesitate to add the sentences of the Creed. One could consider taking the Creed, for example, for the first week or the first half of the month during which time the other meditations are set aside. Then perhaps, it will be discovered that something like a dialogue occurs between the two meditations. They can support and fructify one another as can other variations. The Creed should have a firm place in one's spiritual activity for a lifetime — not lie in the corner of a drawer. It should have a place in our lives, in our hearts. For this to happen we must ever anew turn to the content.

When someone becomes a member of The Christian Community, he is given a copy of the Creed for his own meditation to travel the path which leads to becoming a Christian with the help of the twelve sentences. Yet all spiritual work will only have a Christian meaning if I do it not merely for myself. (This is, of course, also true for work in the external world.) In the Lord's Prayer this is readily understandable: For I can only speak the 'Our' seriously if I involve at least one other human being in the prayer. Speaking and contemplating the Creed also has a meaning extending beyond myself. By uniting myself with the Creed, I unite myself with the power which lives in The Christian Community. I participate in this power and at the same time make it stronger. A picture for this would be a boat which is occupied by many rowers, all of whom participate in the common rhythm and at the same time through their efforts increase the power and speed of progress through the water, for the individual, and for all.

Those who take the Creed into their spiritual activities may say to themselves: I want to do this with, and for the strengthening of, the community in which I live. Then the reading of the Creed in the Act of Consecration of Man after the Gospel is a genuine expression of the community of will, of spiritual activity, of all those present, participating in the confession to that which is revealed through Christ.

Much has remained unsaid in this introductory book. Also much of what could have been said has perhaps not yet occurred to the author. The joy of discovery remains open for the individual reader.

The Apostles' Creed

I believe in God the Father almighty,
creator of heaven and earth;

and in Jesus Christ,
his only son,

our Lord,

who was conceived by the Holy Spirit,
born from the Virgin Mary,

suffered under Pontius Pilate, was crucified,
died, and buried,
descended to hell,
on the third day rose again from the dead,

ascended to the heavens,
sits at the right hand of God the Father almighty,
thence will come
to judge the living and the dead.

I believe in the Holy Spirit,

the holy catholic church, the communion of saints,
the remission of sins,
the resurrection of the flesh,
and eternal life.

Amen.

The Nicene Creed

I believe in one God the Father Almighty;
Maker of heaven and earth,
and of all things visible and invisible.
And in one Lord Jesus Christ,
the only-begotten Son of God,
begotten of the Father before all worlds
(God of God), Light of Light, very God of very God,
begotten, not made, being of one substance (essence) with the Father;
by whom all things were made;
who, for us men and for our salvation,
came down from heaven,
and was incarnate by the Holy Ghost,
of the Virgin Mary,
and was made man;
and was crucified also for us under Pontius Pilate;
he suffered and was buried;

and the third day he rose again,
according to the Scriptures;
and ascended into heaven,
and sitteth on the right hand of the Father,
and he shall come again with glory,
to judge both the quick and the dead;
whose kingdom shall have no end.
And (I believe) in the Holy Ghost, the Lord and Giver of Life;
who proceedeth from the Father (and the Son);
who with the Father and the Son together is worshipped
and glorified;
who spake by the Prophets.
And (I believe) in one Holy Catholic and Apostolic Church.
I acknowledge one Baptism for the remission of sins;
and I look for the resurrection of the dead,
and the life of the world to come.

Amen.

Further reading

The Christian Community by Louise Madsen, Floris Books, 1985.

Growing Point by Alfred Heidenreich, Floris Books, 1979.

Why Ritual? by Michael Tapp, Floris Books, 1978.

Seven Sacraments in The Christian Community by Evelyn Capel, Floris Books, 1981.

Baptism by Maarten Udo de Haes, Floris Books, 1985.

Birth by Evelyn Capel, Temple Lodge Press, 1978.

The Path to Birth by Stanley Drake, Floris Books, 1984.

The Act of Consecration of Man by Martha Heimeran, Christian Community Press, 1975.

The Creed by Evelyn Capel, Floris Books, 1985.

Marriage by Adam Bittleston and others, Christian Community Press, 1971.

In the Midst of Life by Evelyn Capel, Temple Lodge Press, 1980.

Death, the End is the Beginning by Evelyn Capel, Temple Lodge Press, 1979.

The Christian Year by Evelyn Capel, Floris Books, 1982.

Biblical Rhythms in Biography by Diether Lauenstein, Floris Books, 1983.

Christianity and Reincarnation by Rudolf Frieling, Floris Books, 1977.

Christianity and Islam by Rudolf Frieling, Floris Books, 1977.

FURTHER READING

The Three Years by Emil Bock, Floris Books, 1980.
Easter by Freidrich Benesch, Floris Books, 1978.
Ascension and Pentecost by Rudolf Steiner, Anthroposo-
    phical Publishing, 1958.